Plan a Fabulous Party

Party

...In No Time

Tamar Love

800 East 96th Street,
Indianapolis, Indiana 46240

Plan a Fabulous Party In No Time

International Standard Book Number: 0-7897-3221-1

Library of Congress Catalog Card Number: 2004107602

Printed in the United States of America

First Printing: November 2004

07   06   05   04   4   3   2   1

Trademarks

Warning and Disclaimer

Bulk Sales

Que Publishing offers excellent discounts on this book when ordered in quantity for bulk purchases or special sales. For more information, please contact

U.S. Corporate and Government Sales
1-800-382-3419
corpsales@pearsontechgroup.com

For sales outside of the U.S., please contact

International Sales
international@pearsoned.com

Executive Editor
Candace Hall

Development Editor
Lorna Gentry

Managing Editor
Charlotte Clapp

Senior Project Editor
Matthew Purcell

Production Editor
Jessica McCarty

Indexer
Chris Barrick

Technical Editor
April-Dawn Shinske

Publishing Coordinator
Cindy Teeters

Designer
Anne Jones

Cover Designer
Nathan Clement, Stickman Studio

Page Layout
Brad Chinn
Stacey Richwine-DeRome
Julie Parks

Contents at a Glance

Table of Contents

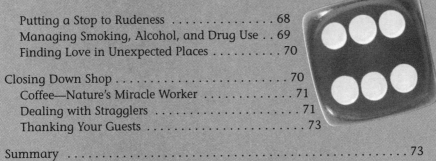

II The Perfect Party

III Variations on a Theme

IV Party Planning Tools

About the Author

Tamar Love is a freelance writer and editor with eight years of professional experience. In addition to writing regular features for Tana's Habitat, a do-it-yourself/lifestyle website for Generations X & Y, Tamar writes and edits for Random House and Chronicle Books and runs Cranky Editor (www.crankyeditor.com), her editorial services company.

For many years, Tamar was a food writer and literary arts editor at SF Station (www.sfstation.com), an alternative web guide to the city of San Francisco. Tamar was also a staff writer for About.com, worked the news desk at *Wired News*, and wrote features for the *San Francisco Examiner*, CitySearch, and MyPleasure.com. Other clients have included *Time Out* travel guides, Food First environmental publishing, Ten Speed Press, and The Sharper Image. She has edited three books on etiquette.

Tamar received her Master of Arts in creative writing from San Francisco State University in 2000. A resident of the Bay Area for almost a decade, Tamar now lives in Burbank, California with her husband, cats, and dogs.

Dedication

I would like to dedicate this book to the memory of my father, Robert Read Love (1944–2004), who was a most excellent father to me for 34 years and an outstanding husband to my mother, Kathleen Love, for 38 years. We miss you, Dad.

Acknowledgments

I would like to thank the many friends, family members, and colleagues who contributed recipes to this book: Bambi Alexander Banys (My Beans); Satarupa Bhattacharya (Limoncello); Lauren Briskin (Beer Cake); LeAnne Brogan (Top of the Morning Banana Bread); Amy Cousland (Shashlik the Molokan Way); Heather Davis (Dee's Bean Dip); Stephanie Garrabrant-Sierra (Iptacita's Guacamole); my late grandmother, Shirley Hackbarth (Grandma's Chicken Wings, Grandma's Sauerbraten); Laurel Hodghead (KKL's Grilled Asparagus); Raquel Jones-Pierce (Eggs Fantastic); Amy Kiser (Yam-chiladas); Cindy Rokicki (Cindylicious Aioli); Thomas Lloyd and Theresa Serna (Carnitas); Kathy Love (Mom's Strawberry Trifle, Mint Chocolate Pie, Seven-Layer Traveling Taco Dip, Mom's Famous Tri-Tip Roast with Gravy); Liana Padilla (Mango Salsa, Cranberry Cocktail Punch Cooler); Jennifer Rutan (Killer Broccoli Salad); Carole Lynn Sokoloff (Low-Carb Cheesecake); Erica Sokoloff (Erica's Favorite Salad); Chris Stratton (Personal Grilled Pizza); Carrie Wilksen (Terry Wilksen's Summer Salad); and Kristin Zwart (Kristin's Balsamic Vinaigrette).

Thanks to Saadia Billman for writing down the rules to "Miss Betty's Dice Game," which everyone who reads this book must play at least once in his or her life. For acting as a general sounding board and givers of great advice, dog and otherwise, thanks to the folks at 3338 (you know who you are). Thanks also to Tana March, whose website (www.tanashabitat.com) published my first party-planning article. Huge thanks to Candy Hall, my editor at Que Publishing, for finding me and making me write this book. I must thank my family, including my grandmother, who reads everything I write with much happiness, and especially my mother, who (as she keeps reminding me) made me.

Finally, I must give the biggest thanks of all to my husband, Carl Grande, for putting up with me while I wrote this book. I'm sorry I was such a witch, sweetie—ILY.

Tell Us What You Think!

As the reader of this book, *you* are the most important critic and commentator. We value your opinion and want to know what we're doing right, what we could do better, what areas you'd like to see us publish in, and any other words of wisdom you're willing to pass our way.

You can email or write me directly to let me know what you did or didn't like about this book, as well as what we can do to make our books stronger.

Please note that I cannot help you with technical problems related to the topic of this book, and due to the high volume of mail I receive, I might not be able to reply to every message.

When you write, please be sure to include this book's title and author as well as your name, email address, and phone number. I will carefully review your comments and share them with the author and editors who worked on the book.

Email: feedback@quepublishing.com

Mail: Candace Hall
Executive Editor
Que Publishing
800 East 96th Street
Indianapolis, IN 46240 USA

For more information about this book or another Que Publishing title, visit our website at www.quepublishing.com. Type the ISBN (excluding hyphens) or the title of a book in the Search field to find the page you're looking for.

Introduction

When I was a kid, we seldom had company over, and my mother *never* threw parties. Although she'd followed the pre-inflation life path of many women in the late 1950s and '60s by majoring in home economics in high school (yes, they had majors in high school back then), she absolutely hated entertaining. She cooked beautifully: moist, juicy turkey at Thanksgiving, dozens of unique cookies at Christmas, a home-baked ham at Easter, and nutritious, home-cooked meals all year long. However, all this cooking was "wasted" on just my father and me—and a few relatives on holidays.

I grew up attending other people's parties, wondering why we never had any of our own. Sure, I'd get a small birthday party or two, but nothing like my other friends had: roller-rink birthday parties, group outings to the park, and sleepovers with 12 or more girls. I felt woefully neglected!

It wasn't until I was an adult that I realize *why* Mom hated entertaining so much. It's hard work! Invitations, menu planning, shopping, decorating, cooking, hosting, cleaning up—and you have to be charming and gracious the whole time. The real kicker, though, is the expense. Parties can eat a hole in your budget, often costing far more than you'd planned. There really isn't a lot to get excited about—I can see why Mom preferred to be a guest!

However, parties don't have to be a royal pain and a financial drain. It *is* possible to entertain on a budget, even if you have a busy schedule and limited experience with cooking and hosting. I learned to do it, and so can you.

My friends first dubbed me "cruise director" many years ago, because my favorite thing to do is organize events. I love to have friends over for dinner parties, throw picnics at the park and on the beach, organize group outings to restaurants and other entertainment venues, and launch reading groups and craft parties. To me, the more the merrier! The only problem is that when more people are involved, the work gets that much harder. To become a successful cruise director, you have to learn a few basic skills.

What *Plan a Fabulous Party In No Time* Is About—and What It Is Not

The *In No Time* series was created for busy people who want to develop certain skills or tackle a long-overdue project, but who don't have a lot of time or money to spend on complex processes and complicated directions. The series title has two meanings: You want to spend very little time planning and throwing your party, and you don't have a lot of time to figure out how! This book will address both aspects of the *In No Time* series goal, giving you simple instructions in a quick, concise format you can breeze through in no time.

If you want to learn to become a professional event planner, a master chef, or a fabulous interior decorator, you will find many detailed books on these subjects; however, this is not one of them! *Plan a Fabulous Party In No Time* is not a detailed guide to every kind of party imaginable, but rather a concise guide to throwing the *best* party, with ideas about how to adjust the perfect party to almost any scenario.

In a fun and fast format, this book will guide you through different aspects of party planning, including

- Determining your personal party style
- Throwing a fantastic party on any budget
- Deciding the theme for your party and planning accordingly
- Selecting the right location for your party
- Creating ambience with music and décor
- Making a guest list and sending out invitations
- Planning a menu and shopping for the right ingredients
- Preparing ahead for the big day

- Managing your party from beginning to end
- Learning to mind your party Ps and Qs—and helping your guests out of sticky situations
- Dealing with the "after party"
- Ensuring your guests have an utterly fabulous time

Because I taught myself the fastest, easiest, and least expensive way to host gatherings, you'll reap the benefits of my knowledge as you read this book. You won't find any extravagant suggestions or overly complicated instructions, but the very best way to host the very best party for *you*.

Who Should Read This Book

I wrote this book with my friends, family, and colleagues in mind: interesting people with average incomes and moderate culinary skills who love to throw a great party when the mood strikes them. If that description fits you, then you are reading the right book! In more detailed terms, this book was meant for readers who

- Love to throw parties, but find they often spend more time and money than they'd like
- Have never thrown a party before in their adult lives, but are looking forward to learning how
- Have thrown dozens of successful parties, but are always looking for a great tip or a new idea
- Are devoted guests (folks like Mom) who never want to throw a party as long as they live, but love to help their friends and family entertain

Some people will quickly realize that they need more resources than this book provides. For example, if your home is on the messy side, you might want to read a few organizational books and turn your "before" into an "after"—*before* you host your first party. If your cooking skills are nonexistent, you might want to supplement your reading with a basic cooking class. If you don't know the difference between vodka and rum, you'll want to take a tour of your local liquor superstore.

At the end of this book, I've included a number of resources and recommendations for further reading, so don't worry overmuch if you don't understand a particular direction. I promise that this book won't leave you feeling lost in the world of partydom.

How to Use This Book

Although I have written this book from beginning to end, you don't have to read it that way. You *should* read the first few chapters, though, so you can learn some basics about easy entertaining. Once you have mastered the fundamentals, you can skip ahead and read about the type of party you want to host. You'll want to skim through the sections on different kinds of parties, and you'll certainly want to review the appendixes, which contain some important tools for party preparation. However, this book, like all the books in the *In No Time* series, was meant to be a reference guide, not a novel to be read from start to finish (although you will not be penalized for doing so, should you wish!).

This book is divided into four main parts:

- **Part I: Know Your Party Self** shows you how to differentiate the kinds of parties that fill you with joy from those that fill you with dread. You'll learn how to select dates, themes and venues, plan around your budget and schedule, create physical moods that suit different events, plan entertainment and events your guests will love and ensure everyone has a great time—including you!

- **Part II: The Perfect Party** takes you through a complete party, giving instructions on making a specific budget, menu, guest list and shopping list, making a to-do list and planning ahead, managing your many tasks on the day of the party, learning to delegate, guiding your party from the moment the guests arrive to the hour they depart and cleaning up after everyone is gone.

- **Part III: Variations on a Theme** shows you how to incorporate the "perfect party" detailed in Part II into the specific event you want to host: holiday parties, occasion parties, and theme parties, providing menu suggestions, entertainment and activities ideas, and decorating themes for each type of party.

- **Part IV: Party Planning Tools** includes kitchen equipment, pantry products, foods for the refrigerator and freezer, and other essentials you should have on hand to prepare for any party. You will also find tools for determining how much food and drink to prepare, budget worksheets, and sample shopping and to-do lists.

On the book's web page, you'll find a More Information box listing the recipes available. I have posted a wide variety of recipes for beverages, appetizers, side dishes, main courses, and desserts, with easy instructions for preparing each dish. Although this site is not meant to be a cookbook, I have included enough recipes to guide you through several parties, after which time you'll be a pro at menu planning and ready to discover your own recipes. To find the recipes, go to www.quepublishing.com and type the ISBN of the book (10-digit number listed next to the bar code on the back of your book) into the search field.

You can use the ideas I've presented exactly as they are written, or feel free to customize them for your own experience, adding personal touches wherever you'd like.

Special Elements and Icons

Throughout this book, you'll find a variety of special elements: lists, sidebars, icons, and other "extras" designed to catch your eye and direct it toward items of special interest relevant to the nearby text.

"To Do" and Shopping Lists

I've included specific lists that will help you manage your time and money better as you count down to the date of the party.

- **"To Do" Lists** help you save time, organizing your tasks into quick lists you can check off as you complete each item.
- **"You'll Need" Lists** help you make sure you have everything you need on hand before you start your preparty tasks.

I've also included a number of special tips, notes, and sidebars, which are designed to bring your focus to different ideas for enhancing your party.

Don't Forget the Details!

Even using this book as a guide, planning and hosting a party involves a million details, many of which can get lost as you strive for party perfection. To help you remember important ideas, I've included five special icons:

Do It Ahead—There is absolutely no reason to become frazzled when you can do so many tasks ahead of time—up to a week or a month, in some cases. Look for the Do It Ahead icon for friendly reminders about tasks that can be taken care of long before the guests arrive.

Penny Pinching—Hey, we're all on a budget—no one knows that better than me! After years of making ends meet without sacrificing my social life, I've accumulated a number of tips on saving money wherever I can, ideas you'll find next to the Penny Pinching icon.

Quality Counts—Although you have a budget, it doesn't mean your guests have to use paper napkins at a formal dinner (unless you are having a Tacky Party). When quality matters, I'll let you know with the Quality Counts icon.

Healthy Hostess—Although my hostess skills were founded on mid-century teachings, a lot has changed since 1955. I'll clue you in on ways to keep you and your guests healthier by using the Healthy Hostess icon.

Stress Buster—Although a completely stress-free party is every host's dream, it is seldom a reality. You might not be able to alleviate your stress entirely, but you can do a great deal to reduce it. Look for the Stress Buster icon to find out how.

Your Party Style

As you read this book, try to keep your own style in mind. Hosting a party is not about following a series of rules and guidelines, but rather creating an experience you and your guests can both enjoy. If a particular element doesn't work for you, don't worry about it. Do what works for you.

Part 1

Know Your Party Self

Know Your Party Style

1

T he key to throwing a stylish party is knowing your party style. Yes, we would all like to think we can throw splendid fêtes, replete with champagne, impeccably arranged floral bouquets, hand-lettered place cards, shining sterling, and *haute cuisine*, amidst which the sprinkling of lively chatter confirms your carefully selected guests are toasting you as the hostess du jour.

Many people can actually pull off such magnificence. However, some of us are pretty darned happy with a semi-successful pizza party. Fortunately, this book can help you with both types of parties—and everything in between.

Before you even attempt to throw a party, do yourself— and your guests—a favor and figure out what kind of event suits you best. A good place to start is with this chapter, where you learn a few basics about planning a party that matches your style *and* budget.

In this chapter:

* Determine what kind of party best suits your personality as a host: classy, kitschy, modern, traditional, casual, or formal

* Learn how you can throw a fabulous party whatever your budget—none, some, or way too much

To do list

- ☐ Determine how much effort you are likely to invest in planning and hosting parties
- ☐ Consider your favorite party "flavor"—formal or not-so-much
- ☐ Decide whether you prefer your parties to be traditional or trendy

What Kind of Host Are You?

Ask yourself a question: Do you prefer sit-down dinners or casual barbecues? Be honest. Not everyone loves to give a fully catered sit-down dinner for 20. Although eating in elegance can be a real pleasure, so can toasting your own dessert-on-a-stick over a blazing fire.

Many hosts might not consider throwing a party unless they were able to arrange for a karaoke machine, Japanese food, and a full sushi bar—although other hosts might be horrified at that sort of party, much preferring the understated chic of a martini bar, personalized cocktail napkins, and a jazz trio.

Similarly, not everyone wants to rack her brain for a super-creative party theme—why not just give a dinner or cocktail party? People love those!

There is no right or wrong party style. If you put your personality into a party, you're going to be a success. The key is figuring out what suits you, and then putting your heart into throwing the very best party you can.

Although you might aspire to be Hostess of the Year, don't take on a huge project unless you have the time, money, and energy to do so. Your friends won't disrespect you for hosting low-key affairs—they'll respect you for being fabulous at something at which you are really good.

You'll Need

- ☐ The ability to honestly assess your personal preferences

Time and Money: Formal Versus Casual

If you love planning and executing elegant affairs, complete with numerous floral arrangements, elaborate décor, haute cuisine, and table settings that rival those in the Ritz Carlton's dining room, you are a *formal* host. If you prefer to keep things simple—a great barbecue, uncomplicated décor, and some good friends lounging in the backyard—you a *casual* host. Most of us are somewhere in between, but it is good to know the direction in which you lean and plan accordingly.

Ask yourself two questions: How much work do you want to do? How much money can you afford to spend? Although a fair amount of cash and effort go into hosting a casual party, a successful formal party requires more abundant quantities of time and money.

Think about formal parties you have attended, such as a wedding reception, large dinner party, or banquet. Although you may have had a wonderful time, you doubtlessly noted that the scope of the event was much grander than a simple cock-tail party or mixer. The hostess may have seemed smiling, relaxed, and radiant, but she had to expend a great deal of effort to throw her fabulous party.

Now think about the more casual get-togethers you have attended, such as an open house, birthday party, or backyard barbecue. Although the host probably spent valuable time and money in making the experience fun and comfortable for every-one, his efforts weren't nearly as complex as those of our formal hostess.

Chances are good that you enjoyed yourself at both types of parties, but what you really need to determine is how much fun you'll have *hosting* either party. Some peo-ple absolutely adore throwing large, scrumptious formal parties, and others shudder at the thought. Decide which you prefer, and focus on throwing those types of parties.

Of course, it's entirely possible that you enjoy hosting formal *and* casual parties. In this case, let your schedule and budget dictate which type of party you select. If you have a huge budget and a lot of free time, by all means put both to good use and throw a huge, elaborate gala. However, if you are like most of us, you're always looking for ways to save time and money. In this case, opt for more casual parties—or throw formal parties for fewer people.

If you're dying to host a formal dinner party, but you just don't have the time or money, consider a formal dinner party for four people. You'll experience the same pleasure of preparing a five-star meal and gussying up your home, but you won't expend as much time or money as you would for a larger formal party.

Keep in mind that even traditionally formal events, such as the aforementioned wedding receptions, banquets, or dinner parties, can be thrown with a casual spirit. If the bride does not have an easy schedule or a large budget, she can get creative, hosting a fun picnic or cocktail party instead of a formal reception. Likewise, a host with plenty of time and money can formalize a traditionally casual event, such as an open house or barbecue, by providing sumptuous extras, including a full bar, haute cuisine, and elaborate decorations.

Please note that "casual" does not entitle you to be "cheesy." Expect to purchase the same quality of food you would provide at a formal party: extra-lean meats; fresh, healthy vegetables and fruits; and an assortment of appetizers that stimulate the palate. Even if your budget is small, you can still provide appetizing fare for your guests. No delivery pizza, please!

Attitude: Classy Versus Kitschy

If Villeroy & Boch china, Waterford crystal, and Tiffany flatware all make you swoon, you are a *classy* hostess. If you prefer Fiestaware dishes, vintage barware, and eclectic, mismatched cutlery, you are a *kitschy* hostess. Similarly, if dinner parties, wedding showers, and open houses are your speed, you are a *classy* host. If you opt for scavenger hunts, disco parties, or tiki barbecues, you are a *kitschy* host.

If *formal* and *casual* denote budget and the amount of work you are willing and able to put into a party, *classy* and *kitschy* are all about attitude.

Classy hostesses are generally adept at throwing formal dinner parties, but also can pull off an outstanding costume party, neighborhood scavenger hunt, or block party. Kitschy hostesses can be equally adroit at kicky casual barbecues, cocktail parties, or high teas. It's all about combining attitude with effort.

Again, "kitschy" does not mean "low-class." Kitsch is all about fun, frolic, and style, which usually means you found the items at a great bargain. Cute vintage items should be clean and in good repair.

note   One of the most interesting parties I ever planned was a formal hoedown for a wealthy client's 60th birthday celebration. Without any real budget or time constraints, I was able to pull out all the stops. I reserved a ballroom in a posh hotel and rented movie-quality set pieces: bales of hay, farm tools and machinery, Western storefront and hitching-post simulations, faux barnyard animals, and even a scarecrow! Although I employed an excellent caterer, I kept the menu simple: roasted pork and chicken, barbecued beans, corn bread, corn on the cob, and a few other side dishes and desserts. I used fun, cowboy-themed décor for the table settings, and guests were informed that they needn't bust out the black ties or gowns, that casual—or cowboy!—attire was perfectly fine. The end result of this juxtaposition of formal and casual? Many of the guests confided that this was the best party they'd ever attended.

What does this anecdote prove? Well, even though the party had a casual atmosphere, the formal aspects (venue, food, décor, budget, and effort) defined my approach to planning the party. Had I been a casual party host, the event would not have been as successful.

Creativity: Modern Versus Traditional

Is your favorite kind of party a structured affair, or do you like fun, quirky theme parties?

Although the word *traditional* might have negative connotations for some people (boring, "been there, done that"), in the context of this book, it is anything but negative. Traditional hosts excel at sending out printed invitations, planning a swank buffet, coordinating entertainment, and providing a variety of beverages—everything you might expect when you think of the word *party*. Traditional parties have worked well for years, so why add a bunch of potentially explosive variables?

Modern hosts love to add excitement to tradition, mixing things up with personal touches. A modern party might consist of eclectic food served in nontraditional surroundings—a Cuban-Vietnamese fusion barbecue in the park—or other spicy touches, such as a funky theme, a diverse group of people, or out-of-the ordinary entertainment or activities.

Most people are not quite as easily defined as these categories might suggest. Can a traditional hostess throw a formal, kitschy party? Sure! A sit-down dinner (with printed invitations) followed by a Miss Betty's Dice Game would suit this hostess perfectly. Likewise, someone who considers himself a casual, classy, modern host would have a great time throwing a cocktail party with Asian finger food and a martini bar.

Don't be afraid to mix up the different aspects of your personality and reflect them in the parties you give. Remember: Creativity, effort, and attitude are the key elements to throwing a party that really works. Know how much of each quality you want to utilize, and you'll have no problems finding the kind of party that suits your style.

Determining your party style is the *very first thing* you should do before proceeding further into this book or with planning your party. Take a moment to reflect on your personality, and then continue reading with your decision in mind.

note In Part III, "Variations on a Theme," I'll be giving you ideas for dozens of parties, with recommendations for budget, party date, theme, venue, guest list, invitations, food, drink, tools, décor, entertainment, activities, and favors. Because your personal party style will determine your approach to each of these planning elements, it's crucial that you familiarize yourself with the terms I've outlined previously. Although I will give specific recommendations, you should let your own party personality guide you as you plan your events.

Partying with Your Style in Mind

As I mentioned at the beginning of this section, there is no right or wrong party style. Whether you are formal or casual, classy or kitschy, traditional or modern, it's important that you host a party that reflects *your* style and personality. If you are a casual, classy, modern host at heart, then hosting a formal, kitschy, traditional party will only frustrate you, and you will likely pass that frustration on to your guests. Approach your party planning with a style that feels comfortable and natural to you, and your party will be a huge success.

To do list

- ☐ Learn how even a small budget can yield a fantastic party
- ☐ Maximize a medium-sized budget
- ☐ Go all out with a fancy shcmancy gala

A Party for Every Budget

It might be difficult to believe, but it *is* possible to throw a party for next to nothing. The trick is to plan your party around your budget, not the other way around.

If money is a serious concern for you (and who isn't worried about cash flow?), make every penny count. Save your party funds in separate envelopes, marked "food," "drinks," "entertainment," "décor," and other key categories, and then only use the money you've set aside in those envelopes. You'll force yourself to think creatively about purchasing supplies.

No-Frills Fêtes

Traditionally, low-budget parties have included pay-at-the-door keggers or no-host bars, *sans* appetizers. Although these types of parties are perfectly nice at certain points in our lives, as an adult, you really can do better.

Let's define a low-budget party as one that costs less than $10 per person. To determine how much your low-budget party will cost, simply multiply your projected guest count by the amount you're willing to spend per person, and you'll have your total budget for your venue, invitations, food, drink, tools, décor, entertainment, activities, and favors. If you'd planned to have a party for 50 people, that means you'll spend between $50 and $500.

You'll have to use a little common sense when selecting your actual per-person price for your party. For example, it's going to be tough to spend only $50 on a party for 50 people! However, you can host a wonderful low-budget dinner party for six people on $60.

If you don't have a lot of money to spend, but would like to host a somewhat elegant party, consider inviting fewer guests. For example, I recently threw a party with a budget of $350. Although my intent was to keep the party low-cost, I only wound up inviting 35 people, which meant I was able to spend $10 per person, thus stretching my budget much further than I'd originally thought. My guests reaped the benefits, enjoying sirloin hamburgers and flavored turkey sausage links, instead of the frozen patties and beef links I'd planned.

tip if you're unsure of how much to spend per person, given the wide price range I've established for low-budget parties, consider how much money you really have to spend and divide that sum by your total number of guests. You'll have a good idea of how much money you're spending on each guest, ensuring your no-frills fête is really low-budget.

If you can't spring for a catered affair with a hosted bar and live entertainment, don't despair. Why not try something a little less traditional?

- **Wine and cheese party**—You supply the cheese and the atmosphere, and each guest brings a bottle of wine to share. You'll have a great time pairing your favorite artisan bleu cheese with your friends' favorite vinos, and the potluck theme will ensure you won't spend more than a few dollars per person. Your projected cost: $45 for 15 people.

- **Elegant brunch**—Morning meals traditionally cost less to prepare, so you can go all out creating a graceful menu without breaking the bank. Brunches rarely involve more than a bottle or two of inexpensive champagne (for mimosas), so your booze budget will be nil. Spend a little money on beautiful flowers; set your table with your best linens, dishes, and flatware; and you'll host an affair to remember for relatively little cash. Your projected cost: $100 for 12 people.

- **Small dinner party**—Invite two or three couples; cook a fancy meal with inexpensive ingredients, such as fresh vegetables, grains, and an inexpensive roast; plan a few after-dinner games; and stock the CD player with lively tunes. Most guests will bring a bottle of wine, so you only have to shell out for one or two bottles ahead of time. Your projected cost: $60 for six people.

- **Bowling party**—You make the arrangements with the bowling alley and organize the event, and your guests pay for their own shoe and lane rentals (as you'll indicate on your invitations). Your attitude and your ability to create a fun atmosphere of togetherness and conviviality will keep this Dutch-treat party from seeming like any other bowling night. Your projected cost: $30 for 20 people.

Potlucks or bring-your-own-meat barbecues are other options. If done correctly, your party will be a hit, no matter what your budget. It's all attitude, effort, and creativity!

If you have a little extra to spend, focus on one key element, such as the liquor or the dessert. Purchase a top-shelf vodka or wine, or order something succulent from your favorite bakery, and your guests will perceive your party as pricey and plush.

Midrange Merrymaking

Parties within a midrange budget cost from $11 to $20 per person. Again, that cost should cover everything in your total budget, including venue, invitations, food, drink, tools, décor, entertainment, activities, and favors.

Because you are looking at anywhere from $55 to $1000 for a party for 50 guests, your possibilities for midrange merrymaking are almost limitless. Explore a number of different party combinations:

- **Hosted camping trip**—Rent a campsite at a cushy campground sporting bathrooms, showers, and campsite grills, and invite 10 of your friends. All they'll bring is their own gear, and you'll supply an elegant menu of grilled salmon and corn on the cob, fruit, grilled vegetables, and wine. Your group will have a wonderful, stress-free experience—you will provide the simple menus, and your guests won't have to worry about anything but where they'll sleep. Your projected cost: $150 for 10 people.

- **Chi-chi cocktail party**—Select a few top-shelf liquors and decant the cheap stuff into vintage glass bottles. Make a dozen or so scrumdiddlyumptious appetizers and finger foods, throw on a few "loungey" CDs, dim the lighting, and you're ready to go. Because you have a larger budget, you can also spring for a few extras, such as personalized cocktail napkins and matchbooks—possibly even live entertainment! Your projected cost: $600 for 50 people.

- **Destination Las Vegas!**—Although guests usually pay for their own accommodations and travel when attending a destination party, it doesn't mean you can't go all out. Consider everything else there is to do in Vegas, such as attending shows, taking day trips, renting a fancy car or two for car-pooling in style, or visiting a spa. Although you certainly don't have to pay for everything, you'll be able to pick up the extras, such as tips, several rounds of drinks, transportation, or any other special treats. If you plan a few activities at venues with varying price ranges, you can show your guests a really good time without spending that much money. Your projected cost: $400 for 20 people.

You also can use a slightly larger budget to upgrade your dinner party, arrange a city-wide scavenger hunt, or celebrate the holidays with style. Just keep track of your expenses and make sure you don't go overboard.

Fancy Schmancy

At least once in your lifetime, you will be required to shell out big bucks for a gala event. It might be a graduation party, wedding reception, or post-opera soiree, but the theme will be the same: You will spend more than $20 per person to make the shindig happen.

Fancy schmancy parties don't have to be limited to milestone events; if you have the budget and the inclination, you can celebrate with style as often as you like. Think about one of these substantial events:

- **Formal dinner**—Whether you're celebrating your son's graduation from Harvard or the onset of spring, a formal dinner party is an excellent way to create a stunning memory for all your guests. Hire caterers, servers, designers, and a bartender—you've got the money, now use it! Your projected cost: $500 for 25 people.

- **Vacation "party"**—Arrange for a dozen of your best friends to spend the weekend at a large rental home. Many such properties are available near lush vacation spots, such as in the mountains, at the beach, on a lake, or in the desert (search the Internet, especially off-season), for far less than you might expect. Because you are providing free accommodations, the atmosphere will be convivial the whole weekend, even if you simply grill some dogs. Your projected cost: $750 for 12 people.

- **Golden anniversary party**—Your parents (or grandparents) will only celebrate 50 years of marriage once, so why not go all out? Rent a hotel ballroom, invite everyone they know, and cater the whole thing. Yes, it will break the bank, but it will also shine as the best night in your guests of honor's lives (except the day they got married!). Your projected cost: $2,500 for 100 people.

If you can afford it, hire an event planner for a large, formal party. Yes, after reading this book, you might not think you need one, but if you are busy in your non-party life, you will love having a paid assistant to keep track of all the details.

Because most people reading this book will hover somewhere between no-frills and fancy, the parties I discuss will be aimed at the midrange merrymaking set. However, throughout the book, I'll also give you penny-pinching tips, which will enable you to host almost any kind of party on even a very limited budget. I'll also add tips for upgrading midrange parties with little extras—your event will cost more, but your guests will have a great time!

Summary

In this chapter, you learned a few basics about what kind of parties you are comfortable hosting. You learned that it's possible to host a variety of different kinds of parties that accommodate even the smallest budget. You're off to a great start! In the next chapter, you will learn some basics about party planning: music, food and drink, menu planning, and tools of the trade.

2

Choosing Party Venues

A lot of work goes into planning a party, no matter what the size and scope of your event. You might be surprised to learn that it might require more effort to execute an offsite party than a party at your own home!

Many people limit their hosting to parties they throw in their own homes. Although there is absolutely nothing wrong with home-based parties, a whole world is outside your door, just waiting for you to explore.

In this chapter, we'll cover the basics of selecting a venue, including home-based parties, such as meal or cocktail parties, open houses, or block parties, destination-based parties at bars, restaurants, and banquet halls—even another city—and outdoor parties at the park or the beach, the woods, the river, or the parking lot of your favorite sports arena.

As any designer will tell you, form and function are interrelated. The type of venue you select will have a significant impact on the party you host, and vice versa. Before you commit to a locale, familiarize yourself with the pros and cons of different venues, and find out what you should expect from each type of party place.

When selecting a venue, keep in mind the varying needs of your guests. Will you need to find out about wheelchair access, handicapped bathrooms, or special parking needs? Will vegetarians find plenty to eat? Try to be respectful of your guests' requests—as a host, it is your responsibility to ensure everyone is comfortable, safe, and happy.

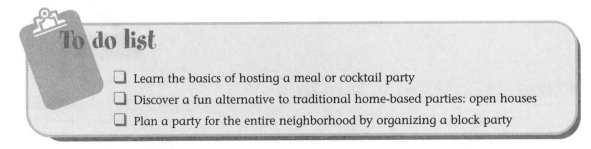

To do list

- ❑ Learn the basics of hosting a meal or cocktail party
- ❑ Discover a fun alternative to traditional home-based parties: open houses
- ❑ Plan a party for the entire neighborhood by organizing a block party

In the House

As I mentioned, home-based events are by far the most common parties given. However, "home party" is a broad category, with several different available options.

Meal and Cocktail Parties

Whether you are throwing a theme or occasion party, the general components will be the same: Guests will come to your house for about four hours, eat and drink, enjoy a little conversation, and then leave—hopefully with smiles on their faces.

The most flexible of all the different types of parties and party venues, home-based meal and cocktail parties are appropriate for celebrating a birthday, anniversary, housewarming party, holiday, special occasion, or almost any other event.

> **tip** Before you begin planning your party, think carefully about where you want to have it. Not all venues are suitable for every party—would you host a children's birthday party at a bar? If you select the venue first, you'll eliminate the need to backtrack and redo any planning you did that won't suit your chosen venue.

- **Pros**—You get to be completely in charge. Not only can you decide the budget, theme, menu, guest list, activities, entertainment, date and duration of the party, but you will also be able to prepare for the party ahead of time, in the weeks leading up to the big date. You might also find it easier to have a party in your own home because you will have everything you need in one place. Best of all, hosting a party in your own home means you won't have to drive anywhere!

One other benefit of hosting a party in your home is that you have more options for stretching your hosting dollars. If you're on a tight budget, make the party work for you. Have a potluck, or plan a dessert-only party. Just tactfully let your guests know what to expect, and they will cheerfully comply.

- **Cons**—You have to be completely in charge. You will have to do all the work or delegate tasks to helpers, whom you must then supervise without seeming micro-managerial. You'll also run the risk of damage to your home or personal belongings, and you might have to deal with people who aren't sober enough to drive home. As if all that isn't enough, you'll be stuck with all the guests for the entire evening, until the very last person goes home.

Of course, hosting a home-based party means you'll need to have a home to which you're comfortable inviting people. Whether you're planning a sit-down dinner, a stand-up mixer, or a backyard barbecue, your home will be the focus of your guests' attention. Make sure it is clean, uncluttered, and comfortable, with plenty of extra toilet paper!

> **tip**
>
> When you're planning your home-based party, think about how long you'd like it to last. Although an all-nighter is certainly testament to your hosting skills, you might need to get up early the next day. When you're ready to close up shop, brew a pot of coffee. Your guests will get the hint.

Open Houses

A variation on the traditional house party, an open house offers guests the opportunity to drop in when it is convenient for them. Generally scheduled as daytime affairs lasting from five to eight hours, open houses require the same amount of planning as a regular home party, but are less structured, enabling you to accommodate your guests' different schedules, especially around holidays.

A popular way to announce yourself in a new neighborhood, open houses are also great for graduation parties, holiday parties, and any other occasion when guests might have several things to do on a given day. As the name of the party suggests, you are opening your home to guests, who might need to arrive at different times throughout the day and stay for only a few minutes or up to a few hours.

- **Pros**—You won't have to pay much attention to the progression of your party. At your open house, you'll block out a period of time for the party, during which time guests can come and go as they please. You won't have any activities or entertainment to plan, so all you'll really need to moderate on the party day is your available levels of food and drink. Because you won't be consulting your watch as often, ensuring your party is progressing as planned, you might even have a little more time to socialize!

- **Cons**—Because open houses generally run the whole day, you'll need more sustained energy to last out the party. You'll spend more time on greetings and goodbyes, which means you'll need to remain friendly and flexible all day, in top form, regardless of how tired you might feel by Hour Six.

If you'd like to host an open house, plan enough food and beverages for each invited guest, plus about 10% more. As people drop by, they'll often have additional friends and family with them. Remain flexible and cheerful, welcoming additional guests with a smile.

Open-house fare typically includes plenty of appetizers, beverages and desserts, but no home-prepared main course, such as grilled food. Because the party is set up to accommodate guests coming and going all day, the food will need to be ready at zero hour and the platters replenished all day long.

If you'd like to include something heartier, cook or purchase a dish that will be ready to serve and remain delicious (and safe to eat) throughout the life of your party. A precooked, honey-glazed ham or a deli-meat platter can both be safely served cold and will accommodate a large number of guests.

> **tip** Make sure your guests understand the nature of your party! Include a bit of text on your invitations that indicates your open house will last from noon to 6:00 p.m., asking guests to stop by any time during those hours.

Block Parties

Similar in scope to an open house, block parties take everything outdoors, expanding the ease and relatively low expense of potluck meals to a neighborhood scale. Second-tier national holidays, such as Independence Day, Memorial Day, Halloween, or Veterans Day are popular celebrations for block parties, but you can really have one whenever you want—why not have a spring or summer block party?

- **Pros**—A fantastic way to get to know your neighbors, block parties are fun for everyone, including kids and pets. You'll be near your own home, to which you can retreat when you need a break, and you won't be responsible for much more than your share of the logistical details, a few dishes you'll contribute, and keeping an eye on your family members.

- **Cons**—Because block parties are planned and executed by the whole neighborhood (save a few sourpusses who refuse to get involved), you will need to plan this party by committee, which can be harrowing. Also, because the party involves your neighbors (along with any guests you invite), you won't be partying with friends,

> **tip** Although a block party is planned by committee, you'll want one person to act as a moderator, keeping a checklist of what needs to be done: food, rentals, permits, inviting the neighbors, and establishing ground rules. Diplomatically allow the group to suggest the checklist items, wait for different people to volunteer for their preferred tasks, and then assign a date by which the task should be completed.

family, and colleagues inasmuch as you'll be spending the day interacting with different personalities, not all of which will be to your liking.

If you want to organize a block party, you can expect a few obstacles you won't experience with other types of parties, such as getting permission from the city to block off the street, renting or locating enough tables and grills for everyone, delegating efforts to different households, and ensuring everything goes smoothly.

As soon as the idea for a block party begins to surface, immediately investigate your community's particular regulations for such events. Permits can take time to process, so start early.

ATMOSPHERE IS EVERYTHING

At a dinner party I attended many years ago, the hostess served great food: home-made fajitas, fresh margaritas, and even a flan for dessert. Did I have a good time? Sort of. Although she had taken great pains to ensure we'd eat well, that was the extent of her hostessing. Where was the music, the festive Mexican décor?

Before I am judged as a peevish party guest, it's important to know that the air of festivity that usually graces such events was also absent. It was as if the hostess had been so focused on making dinner that she had forgotten she was throwing a party. A little ambience could have kindled a fire within her—zing that might have made her party a total success.

Lest you accidentally become a lame-duck host, please remember the importance of creating atmosphere. You can get away with bargain booze and simple vittles—as long as your party environment is rich and lush, your guests will have a fabulous time and sing your praises.

To do list

- ☐ Learn the rules for hosting a party in a bar or restaurant
- ☐ Decide if you'd like to host a party in a banquet hall or other large venue
- ☐ Discover destination parties, wherein you and your guests party in another city, state, or country

Out of the House

Although hosting a party removed from your home presents its own unique challenges, you will also reap incredible rewards, such as having help with the party planning and leaving cleanup to someone else. The following sections help you consider a number of options for away-from-home celebrations.

Restaurants and Bars

Restaurants and bars are the second-most popular venue for parties (after the host's home) for good reason. Parties in restaurants and bars, while generally more expensive than home-hosted parties, offer a wealth of amenities, especially when it comes to actually executing the party.

- **Pros**—Although you'll need to put forth a bit of effort in planning the party, someone else will do all the really time-consuming work, such as preparing and serving the food and drink, decorating the venue, and cleaning up. You won't need to monitor the party a great deal because the restaurant or bar staff is excellent at logistics, nor will you need to bring anything extra, unless you're planning additional décor for a birthday or other occasion party. Finally, on the day of the party, all you'll really need to do is show up—with a cheerful attitude and a fat wallet, of course!

- **Cons**—In addition to finding an appropriate restaurant that will accommodate the size and needs of your party, you'll also be responsible making the reservation far ahead of time, keeping track of RSVPs, answering questions ("Should I bring a gift?"), ensuring your reservation is large enough to accommodate last-minute arrivals, and acting as a liaison for the restaurant staff. You might also need to pay an additional fee if your party is large enough to require an entire room or section of the venue. The biggest con, however, is the cost: As the host of a bar or restaurant party, you are responsible for the entire check, including bar costs and tip. If your friends are accustomed to Dutch treat at restaurant parties, you're in luck. Otherwise, custom and etiquette both dictate that if you do the inviting, you also do the paying.

Although the logistics can be a nightmare when you are the middle man, dealing with guests on one end and a third-party vendor on the other, restaurant parties are relatively easy to throw. Guests will have attended a number of such events and for the most part, will understand what is expected of them. They'll come prepared with a gift for the honoree, as well as the occasional bottle of wine.

Appropriate occasions for restaurant or bar parties include birthdays, anniversaries, bon voyage/farewell, retirement, holiday gift exchange, club or sorority/fraternity reunions, and other occasions for which the guest list is fewer than 50 people.

Finding one restaurant that will accommodate all your guests' requirements can be tricky. In addition to allowing for different appetites and dietary restrictions, you also want to ensure that you pick a place whose cuisine and atmosphere everyone will enjoy. Brainstorm a few different places, and then run them by the guest of honor or a few close friends that will be attending. That way, if a guest complains about venue or the menu, you'll at least know you tried your best to find a place that would suit others.

WHO PAYS?

Before you plan a restaurant party, think carefully about how you intend to handle the bill. Emily Post gently insists that the person hosting the party pays for everything. In keeping with this rule of etiquette, if you can't afford to pay for your guests' meal, you cannot give a restaurant party.

This rule is suspended for "co-op" parties, which are generally more casual and involve friends or co-workers celebrating a shower, life milestone, work-related event, or bon voyage. If you are co-hosting such a party and it is being held at a restaurant or bar, your guests will know they will be paying their own way. However, the host(s) will need to be prepared to cover any check shortages.

Finally, consider what precedents have been set within your group at previous restaurant events. Some groups are accustomed to splitting the check at hosted restaurant parties, paying for their own dinner, as well as a portion of the guest of honor's meal, especially at restaurant birthday parties. Other groups are accustomed to the host footing the entire bill, including tip and drinks. In some cases, the host pays for the entire bar tab; in others, everyone pays for his own drinks.

To simplify logistics and lower your bill, ask the restaurant if it can arrange a *prix fixe* menu. By fixing the price of dinners, your guests will automatically receive an appetizer or salad and a dessert, with up to three options for a main course, and you can better control the cost of the event.

Large Venues

If you would like to host a large party with more than 50 people (retirement party, graduation party, wedding reception, significant birthday or anniversary, or family reunion) you'll want to have it at a larger venue, where trained professionals set up, cook and serve the meal, monitor party progression, and clean up everything.

Although banquet halls, hotel ballrooms, and restaurant banquet rooms have traditionally been the places to go when hosting large parties, you might have fun exploring interesting alternatives, such as country clubs, museums, university foundations, galleries, or community centers (senior centers, women's centers, or other public places that offer large rooms for rent). You'll want to find out about amenities at these unique locations; although many such venues might not staff events, they often work with party-staffing agencies, which will facilitate your search for the perfect caterer.

- **Pros**—You don't have to do any of the actual work on the day of the party, and yet you will receive all the kudos for planning a great event. You'll also receive help with much of the planning: Most banquet halls utilize a private staff and provide options for the menu, beverages, décor, entertainment, and other logistics.

- **Cons**—Standard large venues can feel a little "tired," so you might have to put your creativity on overdrive to make your occasion feel unique. You'll also need to make quite a few phone calls when you're looking for the right place, unless you are fortunate enough to have received recommendations from someone trustworthy. Oh yeah, and unless you are planning a corporate event or have made arrangements with your guests, you'll also get to pay for the whole thing.

tip When it's time to settle the bill, cut through the hemming and hawing with a little situational math.

If you are hosting the party, accept the bill with grace, scan it for errors, and note whether or not the restaurant has automatically added a gratuity. For large parties, some venues will automatically add anywhere from 12% to 18% of the total; if you were especially pleased with the service, feel free to add a little more to the tip. If the restaurant did not already add a tip, mentally multiply the pre-tax total by 15%, and then adjust for exceptionally good (or bad) service.

If you are fortunate enough to host a Dutch-treat restaurant or bar party, you will still be responsible for dealing with the bill's logistics. Determine an appropriate tip (if gratuity isn't already included), add it to the total, and divide evenly by the number of persons in your party, minus the guest of honor. If you choose, you can ask guests to contribute less if they didn't drink alcohol and more if they did. Keep in mind that as the host, you are ultimately responsible for the check. If your guests' contributions fall short of the total, it's your job to make up the difference with tact and grace, which means reaching for your own wallet.

PROGRESSIVE PARTIES

If you're especially organized and would like an exciting challenge, try planning a progressive party, one event that takes place over time, at several different locations, with each guest paying her own way.

Although not for the easily flummoxed, progressive parties can be incredibly fun for everyone, even the host. A typical party might flow like this:

- ✳ 6:00 p.m.: Meet at a specific bar for cocktails.
- ✳ 7:30 p.m.: Move to a pre-designated restaurant for dinner.
- ✳ 9:30 p.m.: Head out to a cafe for dessert and coffee.
- ✳ 10:30 p.m.: Boogie on over to a dance club or bar featuring live entertainment.

Progressive parties can also take place at several different homes:

- ✳ 6:00 p.m.: Meet at Bill's house for cocktails and appetizers.
- ✳ 7:30 p.m.: Move to Doug and Sharon's house for dinner.
- ✳ 9:30 p.m.: Head over to Cindy's house for dessert and coffee.
- ✳ 10:30 p.m.: Finish up at Blaine and Sarah's house for games.

Although these two events might seem like a typical night on the town, the challenge for the hostess is organizing logistics at the different locations, making sure everyone gets where they are supposed to be at the right time, and imbuing the event with a festive, party atmosphere.

You might throw a progressive party for a bachelorette or birthday party, or you might organize this event to introduce disparate friends to one another.

Substantially more expensive than bar or restaurant parties, banquet-hall parties do ease the burden of planning. You won't have to deal with place settings, calling all over town to find what you need, or actually doing the physical work large parties demand. Yes, you will pay for your status as decision maker, not day laborer, but isn't the reduced effort worth the larger budget?

tip To simplify matters, you might want to consider renting a bus or limousine for the evening; if appropriate, guests can each contribute $20 to defray the cost. Just make sure your guests' expectations are clear from the outset.

If you are on a limited budget, don't feel at all guilty about arranging for a no-host or cash bar, which means that soft drinks are complimentary (or rather, paid for by you), but alcohol is paid for by those who will be drinking it. Again, just make sure to include the words "no-host" or "cash" bar on your invitations so your guests will know what to expect.

> **tip** Instead of renting out an entire banquet hall, ask around at your favorite restaurants, many of which will host large parties in separate rooms. Although you won't have the same staff-to-guest ratio attention from every staff member as you would at a banquet hall, you'll save a lot of money and you might get better-quality food.

Destination Parties

As the name suggests, destination parties take place away from your home, often occurring at a vacation spot or remote city. Although not appropriate for every kind of party, destination parties are great for celebrating marriages, family reunions, significant birthdays or anniversaries, or important holidays.

- **Pros**—Having all your friends and family in one location can be really fun! During meals and activities, you'll have ample opportunity to reconnect with people you might not have seen in a while. By spending several days together, you'll fall into a comfortable routine, not only spending time with other guests, but taking time out for yourself and/or your partner.

- **Cons**—Destination parties can be incredibly expensive logistical nightmares. You'll need to plan accommodations, help with travel, arrange meal and activity options, and make sure guests understand payment arrangements. Although you don't have to pay for the entire event, you will need to cover any "unclaimed" costs, such as a short hotel or restaurant bill or rental fees for group activities.

Given the nature of destination parties, your guests will certainly not expect you to pay for their travel or accommodations, unless you specify that the entire event will be on you. This financial arrangement might make you feel less than a hostess, so be sure to make all the arrangements for your guests, which will keep them feeling like guests, and not as if you're merely meeting up at a common destination. If you're planning a party in a different city, arrange for a block of hotel rooms— perhaps even at a reduced rate!—and make reservations for shows, activities, or other special events that allow your group to party en mass.

Another way to look at destination parties is as a "vacation" party, in which you rent a home at a getaway locale, such as a river or beach or in the mountains. Such rental properties often cost far less than you might imagine, lending a festive, party

air to the group vacation. Your guests will probably reciprocate by taking you out for whatever
group meals you haven't planned and cooked
yourself.

Are destination parties worth the effort? Well, you
will have to put a great deal of effort into organizing the event, but all that hard work will definitely pay off when you rekindle relationships
with friends, family, and college or high-school
buddies.

Many websites offer tools for organizing large
parties traveling to a common destination. Guests
can log on and find different options for accommodations, travel, meals, and activities, making
their own arrangements. Wedding websites, such
as www.theknot.com, are great for this type of
service, but a quick Google search will yield additional results in your area.

note Destination
parties can
be tricky if you expect children,
seniors, or disabled people to attend. Keep
your guests' needs in mind when you select
your spot, and try to pick a destination that
will accommodate everyone in your party.

tip Ask your travel agent if she will
help you plan your destination
party. For a relatively small fee, many agencies will help with accommodations, travel,
transfers, meal arrangements, and
activities.

To do list

- ❑ Learn about the different logistics that apply to parties at the park, beach, or elsewhere in the great outdoors
- ❑ Discover tailgate parties, which don't have to be limited to sports enthusiasts
- ❑ Find out how to turn a camping trip into a fabulous party

The Great Outdoors

I remember my first outdoor party, a Memorial Day picnic at Golden Gate Park. We
spent about eight hours at our reserved site, grilling burgers and hot dogs; greeting
guests as they arrived throughout the day; and playing badminton, kickball, and
Scrabble. Toward the end of the day, as the sun began to set, a feeling of frivolity
prevailed, and I felt like a little kid, zooming around the field before Mom called me
to come inside. I can only hope your experiences with outdoor partying are as good
as mine. But you won't know until you try, will you?

If you decide to host an outdoor party, remember that you and your guests will be at the whim of the weather. Although you can try to be proactive and check the weather report, you never know when you'll be thwarted by an unexpected rainstorm, tornado, or flock of angry geese.

Be sure to remind your guests that they will need to take precautions against the sun and the weather. Although applying sunscreen is now second nature for many people, you'll want to remind them to slather it on. Likewise, you might want to remind them to bring an umbrella or a sweater in case inclement weather arises.

The Park

Perhaps the easiest locale for an outdoor event, the park is ready-made for picnics, barbecues, and luaus. Yes, you'll need to bring your own food and supplies, but you'll generally have access to one or more picnic tables, a grill, and, most important, bathrooms. A park is a safe, relatively comfortable outdoor locale for your first—or 40th!—outdoor event.

- **Pros**—Most people are centrally located to a great city or state park, which means minimal travel time for you and your guests. Aside from the aforementioned amenities, parks offer built-in entertainment: feeding the ducks, strolling along paths, admiring the foliage, and playing dodgeball.
- **Cons**—Parks also contain other people's children, bees, and the occasional pervert, none of which are particularly fun to be around. Parks can also be crowded, especially on national holidays, and parking can be a problem, particularly if you have to haul your gear a mile from the parking lot.

Although a park party can be a casual affair, don't forget to take care of necessary arrangements. If you'd like to plan a park party, call the ranger's office to ensure you have a reservation. Nothing is sadder than arriving at the park to find your selected spot has already been taken by someone with the foresight to make a reservation.

tip If you plan to grill at the park, make sure you bring not only charcoal briquettes, lighter fluid, and matches, but also tools for cleaning the grill before you cook, as well as cleaning up the hot ashes when the party is over.

YOU CAN TAKE IT WITH YOU

Outdoor revelry has its own set of challenges, and a good hostess will plan accordingly. Yes, it would be nice if your guests brought everything they needed to enjoy the event, but as the hostess, it's your job to make sure you have the following:

* Several bottles of waterproof sunblock
* Aloe vera gel
* Insect repellant
* Pre-moistened towelettes (baby wipes are perfect)
* Toilet paper (you never know!)
* First aid kit, including a pain reliever and antihistamine for allergy sufferers
* Matches
* Corkscrew and bottle opener
* Ice chest with plenty of ice
* Collapsible chairs
* Tablecloth
* Picnic blanket
* Grill, charcoal, and lighter fluid
* Extra paper plates, napkins, cups, and cutlery
* Trash bags
* Frisbee, soccer ball, a puzzle, and/or travel-sized games
* Blankets or sweaters for when it cools down
* Wildlife guide book
* Binoculars
* Camera, with extra batteries and film

Yes, your friends might mock you for being over-prepared; taunt them by holding the aloe vera gel just out of reach when their sunburn begins to itch.

Finally, using a web-based invitation system, such as www.evite.com, is a great way to make sure you don't wind up bringing all the gear. Ask your guests to volunteer for a particular tool and/or foodstuff, and then sign up when they RSVP on the website.

Tailgate Parties

Traditionally given before sports events, tailgate parties can really work for any occasion when you find yourself waiting near the back of your car for extended periods of time. Going to the swap meet or flea market at the crack of dawn? Start things right with a breakfast party in the trunk of your car. Amusement-park forays, conferences, or cat or dog shows—any offsite event that does not provide delicious food is ripe for a tailgate party before, during, or even after the event.

- **Pros**—Really, really fun! There's something naughty about foiling the cruelly expensive concession-stand vendors by eating gourmet chow you brought yourself. Let the *joie de vivre* spill over to the rest of your party, and giggle like schoolchildren as you drink 40-ouncers from a paper bag.

- **Cons**—The odor of gasoline might add an unpleasant flavor to your artisan goat cheese marinated in olive oil and herbs. Also, you'll need a bathroom sooner or later, so the call of nature might mean the end of your party.

Although they are usually short and sporadic in nature, tailgate parties are easy to arrange: Just ask each passenger in your car to bring a different dish, à la potluck dinner. You'll need minimal prep time or equipment, and the décor will be the glorious parking lot surrounding you.

You can make the tailgate party experience less "exhausting" by strategically locating your car. Gasoline really isn't healthy to breathe for extended periods of time, so try to park your tailgate party near the edge of the parking lot, which will slightly reduce the fumes.

Although tailgate parties are by nature very casual and spontaneous feeling, excellent food is almost mandatory. Because you are saving money on so many party elements, you can afford to splurge for great cheese, quality meats and breads, and an exotic salad or vegetable. These small luxuries will turn an ordinary event into a splendid little gala.

tip With a little planning, you can stock your vehicle with everything you need for an instant tailgate party, wherever you are. In a small, plastic storage box, pack a blanket, premoistened towelettes, a small cutting board, a sharp knife, a corkscrew, and a few plastic cups. Don't forget a trash bag for cleaning up!

The Beach

One of the absolute best places to party, the beach offers instant atmosphere for a variety of events: If a sunny day isn't reason enough to head for the beach with your pals, plan a birthday, graduation, or bon voyage party—really, any kind of celebration fares well near an ocean or lake.

Don't discount a nighttime beach party, which can be incredibly fun. Check the regulations at your favorite ocean-side spot, and make sure that after-dark parties are allowed, as well as bonfires and grilling.

- **Pros**—Beach parties are relatively easy to organize; most people are familiar with the particular requirements for a day at the beach. The beach is just plain fun, hearkening back to the days when the state of your tan was more important than the state of the world.
- **Cons**—Sand. Itchy, wet bathing suits. Sand in the food. Sand in your sunblock. Sunburn. Screaming children. Children kicking sand on you. The potential for water-related accidents.

Even with the notable cons, a day at the beach is unparalleled fun. Have a lobster boil, grill some dogs, pack a picnic, or make it a potluck—food, people, and a few supplies (see the sidebar earlier in this chapter, "You *Can* Take It with You") are all that you really need.

Just remember to apply sunblock at least 30 minutes before you arrive, and then reapply every two hours, or more frequently if you go swimming. You may also want to limit your beach partying to one staffed by a lifeguard, especially if you expect children will attend. Drowning and rip tides are serious realities, even at beaches you might think safe.

If you are packing sandwiches (my family's favorite was tuna salad), prepare your ingredients ahead of time, and then assemble sandwiches at the beach. Keep the meats and cheeses, breads, and vegetable garnishes separated until you are ready to eat, lest you wind up with soggy sandwiches, but you can slice the tomato, meat, and cheese; clean and shred the lettuce; or mix up the tuna salad ahead of time. Just be sure you leave room in your cooler for anything that might spoil, especially the tuna salad.

tip If you live near a beach or lake, save time and aggravation by packing an all-purpose beach bag you can grab at a moment's notice. Fill a straw or fabric tote with a beach towel, sunscreen, a wide-toothed comb, pre-moistened towelettes, a small first aid kit, a hat, and a juicy novel. Just add a bottle of water, and you're ready to party.

Camping

Usually a multiday event, camping mixes the challenges of a destination party with those of a beach party: You're gonna get dirty, and you're gonna stay that way for days; plus, you'll have to coordinate a group of people who probably don't even own a tent, let alone know you're supposed to brush the area clean of rocks before setting one up. Why, then, do this to yourself? Because camping rocks!

- **Pros**—Camping creates a sense of personal empowerment and self-reliance you simply can't acquire from other parties. Yes, you can pitch a tent. You can also string up an outdoor kitchen, dig a privy hole, grill up a salmon fillet, and get a good-night's sleep, even in the woods. Camping also affords the opportunity for campfires, sing-alongs, ghost stories, and lots and lots of giggling.

- **Cons**—In addition to bugs, bears, and things that go creep in the night, camping presents challenges. There is an art to sleeping (and doing other things) in the woods, and if you have not mastered this art, things could become very uncomfortable for you. Also, when you're stuck in the woods (or at the river), the nearest convenience store is usually quite a ways away, which might present problems for the unprepared. Because public campgrounds are, well, public, you'll be in close proximity to other campers, not all of whom you might love. You'll also need to observe all the park rules, including drinking and pet restrictions, quiet hours, and group size.

Campsites fill up quickly, so be sure you reserve yours as far ahead of time as possible. Many state parks will take reservations over the Internet, so Google your state and see what you find. Many such websites offer important information about amenities, as well as a visual layout of the campground, allowing you to select a specific site.

Camping is enough of a challenge without making the experience more difficult than it needs to be. Unless all your guests are seasoned pros, consider selecting a campground that offers bathrooms and showers, evening activities, and ample parking, preferably away from your campsite.

When you call to reserve your campsite, ask the park ranger about any dangers, such as bees, bears, snakes, poison ivy or oak, stinging nettle, or rapid-moving waters. When you extend your

> **tip** If you've never been camping before—or if it's been a long time since your last Boy-Scout camping trip—check your local outdoor-gear store for camping classes. In addition to learning the basics of tent-pitching and cooking in the great outdoors, you'll get inside advice on the gear you'll need to purchase before visiting the great outdoors.

invitations, be sure to let your guests know of these dangers so they can take appropriate precautions.

Also consider the nature of your party: Will your friends prefer to live it up into the wee hours? A camping trip at a public campsite might not be the best choice for you and your pals, unless you enjoy being visited (and kicked out!) by the park ranger. If your friends enjoy good clean fun and are able to limit their giggling to approved hours, then camp away!

A camping trip is in itself a party; do you really need a reason to rough it for a few days? However, if you must find an occasion to celebrate, plan a camping trip for a birthday, reunion, or anniversary.

Summary

In this chapter, you learned how your choice of venue can impact your party, and vice versa. You learned the pros and cons of partying at home, at a restaurant, outdoors, and in other cities. In the next chapter, you'll learn what to do at these venues, and the basics to planning a good party: theme, décor, food and drink, entertainment, and party favors.

3

Party Basics

et's face it—parties are a lot of work! However, just because there is work to do, you don't have to feel overwhelmed. The purpose of this book is to simplify your workload and make complicated tasks easier for you.

With that in mind, this chapter will provide you with valuable information about the basics of hosting, including the value of selecting a theme, planning appropriate decorations for your party, ideas about food and drink, options for different kinds of entertainment, and simple party favors for your guests.

Although we'll cover each subject more thoroughly in Part II, "The Perfect Party," showing you how to plan each element step-by-step, take a moment to become familiar with the different types of planning that goes into hosting a fabulous party.

To do list

- ☐ Learn that holiday parties aren't just for Halloween
- ☐ See that occasion parties don't have to conform to tradition
- ☐ Jazz up your meal parties with simple, silly ideas for fun themes
- ☐ Host a party whose sole purpose is to celebrate a theme

In this chapter:

* Think about incorporating a fun theme into your party shopping list
* Find out about the importance of appropriate décor for your party, whether you have chosen a theme or are keeping things simple
* Understand that food and drink are party essentials, as are the tools you'll need for serving
* Discover that "entertainment" doesn't have to mean a tired game of charades, but can actually be fun for you and your guests
* Learn about fun, inexpensive party favors that will delight your guests

Selecting a Theme

Creating a theme for your party is the simplest way to lend instant atmosphere. Whether your intended effect is kitschy, glitzy, sassy, or classy, selecting a theme will give you the opportunity to *build* a party, instead of just throwing one.

If you're interested in adding a theme to your party, begin by considering what kind of party you want to have. In Part III, "Variations on a Theme," we'll look at different types of parties, many of which can be enhanced with a theme. In this chapter, I'll explain how you can brainstorm these themes, combining tried-and-true and eclectic ideas to produce a party theme that stands out.

Nontraditional Holiday Traditions

If you're planning a celebration for a holiday, use the built-in elements of that holiday to add color to your event. For example, for an Independence Day party, make the event special by incorporating ready-made ideas into your theme: flags; red, white, and blue paper plates and napkins; a rousing game of "pin the beard on Uncle Sam"; and sparklers as party favors.

Christmas, Halloween, and Valentine's Day are easy examples of holidays with built-in theme elements, but you can also explore ideas for lesser-known holidays:

- Want to have a party in April? Earth Day is April 22. Opt for an environmental theme, and play up this international holiday that celebrates environmentalism. Prepare a vegetarian meal, and decorate with environmentally friendly décor (green plants, globes, and recycled-paper products)—you might even make a tree- or garden-planting ceremony part of the party.

- Did you know that September is National Sewing Month? Consider throwing a craft brunch to celebrate this wacky observance. You can decorate with sewing notions, prepare simple fare, and invite your friends over to work on a beginner-level sewing project. You might even use this "holiday" to inspire a monthly craft party!

Because holidays recur every year, you have ample opportunity to stock up long before your next party—and save a ton of money. Shop after-holiday sales at gift, party, and housewares stores, and pick up themed paper plates, napkins and linens, decorations, favors, and other odd items that might come in handy during next year's events.

With a little thought, planning, and creativity, you can turn even the wackiest holidays into fun, quirky celebrations. Look online for a list of little-known observances (www.brownielocks.com/holidayauthenticity.html is a good start!), and let your imagination soar.

Mixing Up Occasion Party Themes

As a trip to any party store will show, birthdays, anniversaries, and other milestone occasions are perfect for theme parties. However, why not get really creative and go beyond traditional milestone themes? "Happy Birthday" balloons are fun for kids, but adults have more sophisticated sensibilities, appreciating eclectic ideas and funky themes. For example

- Instead of throwing a regular birthday party for a friend turning 40, consider throwing a "40s Party" with a swing theme. Prepare food and cocktails appropriate to the era, hire a swing band or stock up on swing CDs, and ask your guests to come in costume. With the recent revival of all things swing, this type of party would be fun and relatively easy to host.

- Incorporate traditional "bon voyage" theme elements into a retirement party or celebration for a friend or co-worker who received a promotion or landed a great new job. Get silly with the planning, including palm trees, beach-themed décor, tropical drinks and food, Hawaiian and beach music, and other elements that convey a similar message: "Say hello to paradise."

As you're considering an upcoming occasion party, let your creativity shape the planning. Mix up elements of traditional milestones, and give your guest of honor a party she won't soon forget.

Serving Up Savory Meal Parties

Perhaps the most frequently thrown types of parties, meal parties focus on the food and drink: breakfast, brunch, lunch, high tea, cocktails, dinner, or dessert. However, although the food is central to the party, you can still incorporate a fun theme to your meal party, giving your guests an event to remember. Consider these ideas:

- Instead of having a casual cocktail party, why not have a disco party? Send out glitzy invites, rig up a disco ball, and throw some '70s tunes in the CD player. Play up the menu with food and drink popular in the 1970s: fondue, meat-and-cheese-based canapés, and powerfully strong cocktails. Costumes are optional, but appreciated!

- Have a high tea or brunch to celebrate spring, inviting guests to a garden party with elegant décor, fresh-cut flowers, an assortment of tea sandwiches (with the crusts cut off!), and a very dignified lemonade punch (spiked with vodka or champagne, if you like). Ask guests to wear their best fancy hats— suggest thrift-store shopping for silly results—or incorporate hat decorating as a party activity, using over-the-top items purchased at a craft store, such as birds, huge flowers, leaves, and dollhouse furniture.

Of course, there's nothing wrong with hosting a simple dinner party, but adding a theme always ups the fun. If you want to keep things simple, adding games to your party and calling it Game Night is an easy way to incorporate a theme without adding much extra planning.

Hosting a Theme-Based Party

Of course, some parties are innately based on themes: costume parties, decade parties, parties based around specific entertainment ideas, or "girly" parties, such as beauty nights, craft groups, or product parties (Tupperware, anyone?).

Some of the best parties are thrown because the host wants to explore an interesting thematic idea. For example

- An entertainment-based party, such as a karaoke, film, or Super Bowl party, in which the theme event is central to the party's concept
- A crafting group, in which guests work on a specific yarn, sewing, or other craft project
- A game night, dice party, or scavenger hunt, at which guests participate in an activity or game

The difference between theme parties and parties that *incorporate* themes is the planning involved. Usually, there is an activity or form of entertainment central to the party's purpose. This activity will have rules or requirements, or built-in ideas about the appropriate types of food, drink, décor, and activities (for example, a Super Bowl party).

As you're planning a theme party, you'll need to determine any specific tools you or your guests will need to supply, directions you need to print up, or special equipment you'll need to buy, rent, or borrow.

Theme parties don't have to break the bank. Shop odd locations for theme-based party supplies, such as your city's Chinatown or another culturally rich area, where you can find clever, inexpensive decorations and favors your guests might find exotic and fun. You'll spend far less than you would at a party-supply store, and the unique details will impress your guests.

Choosing Party Décor

When thinking of party décor, many minds rush straight to streamers and helium balloons. These, however, are not the type of décor to which I refer—unless you are throwing a Tacky Party or a birthday bash for your six-year-old niece.

You won't spend a lot of money or time adding these extras, but your guests will wow over the effort you'll appear to have put into making their night special. By just adding a few details, you'll turn everyday into extraordinary. Instead of focusing on traditional elements, try a little creativity:

- Having a barbecue? Make it a *western barbecue* by covering your tables with red-and-white checkerboard tablecloths, kitschy condiment squeeze bottles, vintage cowboy-printed fabric squares as napkins, and a centerpiece made of chili peppers and Tabasco sauce.
- Planning a martini party? Gussy things up with a *swing* theme: vintage bar glasses, mood lighting in low pinks and yellows, a bowl of cigars, and drink-recipe cocktail napkins.
- Turn an ordinary luncheon into *high tea* by investing in a three-tiered serving platter; linen napkins; clean, polished silver and crystal; and a lovely bouquet of tulips.

Remember to keep safety in mind when you're planning your party décor. Although items sold at deep discounts might be good for your budget, they might not be safe for your guests, especially if you are inviting children. Use common sense: Don't place highly flammable decorative items near open flame, don't use plastic bags or anything with accessible string if you're hosting a party with minors in attendance, and don't encourage guests (especially if they have been drinking alcohol) to toast their marshmallows with short, wooden skewers.

To do list

- ☐ Learn a few basics about menu planning for different types of parties
- ☐ Find out how to calculate the number of drinks you'll need
- ☐ Read up on different tools and skills you'll need to make your party a success

Planning for Food and Drink

Although your menu will change from party to party, one fact remains the same: Your guests will want to eat and drink. Before you get into extensive menu planning, consider a few basics.

FIRE IT UP! CANDLES AND OTHER FORMS OF ILLUMINATION

Even if you cannot afford a single decorative item for your party, you can still create an abundance of ambience just by placing candles around your home. Try a few bright ideas:

* Set floating candles in clear glass bowls filled halfway with water and place in several areas: the living room, the dining room, and, of course, the bathroom.

* Purchase tiki torches (about $5 each, plus citronella oil) and plant them around your front walkway and backyard or patio.

* Arrange pillars of different sizes (but the same color—perhaps white?) into small groupings in areas where guests will be lingering. Feel free to decorate the bases of pillar candles with décor appropriate to your party, such as flowers—just make sure you aren't inviting disaster with a fire hazard. Use new, tall candles, and ensure any décor is far from the flame.

* Dim overhead lighting and cover lamps with sheer, colored scarves. Check your local thrift store for pieces that you might not be caught dead in, but that would look great draped over your too-bright living-room light. Keep safety in mind, ensuring anything draped doesn't touch the light bulb or feel hot to the touch.

* Combine radiance with aroma by lighting assorted scented candles in each room. Keep the flavors the same in each room so your guests don't get overwhelmed by several different odors.

If your budget is extra-tight, don't worry. Candles are inexpensive, especially when purchased in bulk at discount stores or chains that specialize in closeouts.

Save yourself a series of headaches by purchasing several disposable or refillable torch-style lighters and stowing one in each room where candles will burn. During your party, you won't have to search for matches or try to find a lighter that works.

Finally, no mention of candles would be safe without pointing out the dangers of leaving open flames unattended: Don't do it! In the bathroom, leave a candle burning in a fire-safe holder. In other parts of the house, don't light candles at all unless you plan to have guests in those rooms. Check your candles frequently, just to ensure the flame is burning at a safe height, far away from anything flammable. Trim wicks to ¼" before lighting, and make sure the candle wax doesn't spill over onto your furniture or carpet.

Understanding Party Food Basics

Food will probably be the largest, most important variable at any party you host. Although I will go into much greater detail about food later in this book, you should know a few basics about what kinds of food go with what kinds of parties.

- *Standing parties* (cocktail, casual gatherings) call for nibblets and finger foods, and at least six different kinds of appetizers, including dips and sweets.
- At *buffet parties*, plan for one or two main courses (chicken and meat or fish, usually) and up to six side courses, including vegetables, grains, salads, breads, and desserts.
- At *seated parties*, one main course and related side dishes are all that is required, but you will want to serve dinner prefaced by an appetizer and/or salad, and follow it with dessert. Don't forget to have a few pre-dinner noshings available for guests: cheese and crackers, chips and dips, and an additional appetizer or two.

Don't go overboard with food! You might think a sagging table will impress your guests, but if you overdo it, you'll only have leftovers that probably won't keep, as well as an empty wallet. To determine how much food you'll need per person, please consult the Food and Drink Calculator in Appendix B, "Party Tools."

tip Try to keep your menu varied and surprising, but don't make it overly complicated. For example, you might make an exotic main course, but you should pair it with a relatively bland side dish, allowing guests to take a break from spicy flavors. Likewise, spend your time (and money!) preparing one or two significant appetizers, and then round out the menu with dips and breads.

Planning Drinks for Your Party

Although the beverage selection should vary from party to party, a few basic rules hold true:

- Stock up on bottled water and assorted soft drinks (including diet drinks) and juices for guests that don't drink alcohol.

- Make sure you have plenty of ice! A few hours ahead of time, fill a large bucket—or the bathtub!—with ice and chill a selection of soft drinks, beer, and water.
- If you are serving spirits, take into account your guests' varying preferences. Include red and white wine and assorted cocktails.

- Regardless of the event, always have regular and decaffeinated coffee ready to brew toward the end of the night, as well as sugar, cream, and a few interesting coffee condiments, such as cinnamon or vanilla syrup.

Don't forget two critical planning elements with respect to beverages: space and chill factor. Make sure you have enough space in your freezer for the amount of ice you'll need, or plan to hit the store just before the party so the ice doesn't melt before your guests arrive. Also, remember to chill your cold drinks at least 24 hours before the party so that your drinks are deliciously chilled when the guests arrive. You might think you only need a few hours of chilling, but your refrigerator will cool down 80 cans of warm soda more slowly than you might think. You'll need to make room in your refrigerator for all those cans and bottles, too, so keep your cold food requirements in mind.

Although you can't be expected to stock every type of beverage your guests could possibly demand, a good host will have enough of a variety on hand to suit most requests.

> **tip** Although water, juice, and soft drinks are perfectly fine for those who don't drink alcohol, you might also add a few exotic options, such as freshly brewed iced tea, flavored bubbly water, or sparkling juice.

As mentioned elsewhere in this book, you don't have to stock your bar with top-shelf liquor. Keep a few bottles of quality hooch on hand—citron vodka, a good scotch—and decant the bargain liquor into attractive glass bottles. You can also purchase two types of wine: the good stuff for the first hour, and the mediocre stuff for the rest of the night, after the guests have loosened up a little on the quality cabernet.

Basic Tools for Dining and Drinking

No matter what kind of party you're planning, if food and drink are involved (and they'd better be!), your guests will need something from which to drink and eat. You'll need a few basics:

- Paper, plastic, or glass cups from which guests can drink cold beverages; guests will grab a clean glass at least once, so plan accordingly
- Insulated cups or mugs for hot beverages
- Large plates for eating the main meal
- Small plates for desserts and appetizers
- Enough knives, forks and spoons—plastic or metal—so that each guest has a complete set, plus a few extra, just in case

HOW MUCH BOOZE DO YOU NEED?

If you're serving alcohol at your party, how much booze do you need?
Although this subject is covered in greater detail in Appendix B,
it's worth mentioning a little basic math right here:

* Plan for two drinks per person for the first two hours of the
  party, and then one drink per person for every hour thereafter.

* One 750-milliliter bottle of booze (wine, champagne, or liquor) will
  yield about six 4-ounce glasses.

* Plan two cans or bottles of soda per person—change that quantity to three
  if you are hosting a sober party.

* If you're hosting a party heavy on drinks that require ice, such as iced soft drinks
  or blended or shaken cocktails, you'll need ½ pound of ice per person.

Based on the preceding facts, we can calculate the following:

* For a 4-hour party of 20 expected guests, you would plan to serve a total of 120
  drinks.

* To fill glasses 120 times, you will need 20 bottles of booze.

* For this same party, you'll also need 80 cans or bottles of soft drinks or
  water, as well as 20 pounds of ice.

Of course, you can never predict what your guests will want to drink, so don't get
20 bottles of the same liquor! Purchase a mix of red and white wine, champagne, vodka, gin, tequila, rum,
and scotch, plus a few six-packs of quality beer. You might also want to add a few extra bottles of wine, just
in case the party runs late. No need to overdo it, though—many guests will bring a bottle as a hostess gift.

* Twice as many paper napkins as you think you will need (linen napkins are
  great for the table, but guests will need cocktail napkins for drinks and
  appetizers)
* An adequate stash of serving bowls, pitchers, and platters in assorted sizes,
  shapes, and colors
* Any tools you will need to actually serve the food and drinks: large spoons,
  meat forks, a ladle, a corkscrew, a bottle opener, and a carving knife

For more information on recommended party tools, please consult Appendix B.

Thrifty Ways to Stock a Party Closet

Consider starting a "party closet." Similar to the fabled "gift closet," a party closet is a storage container large enough to safely store your party tools: dishes, cutlery, glassware, linens, candles, and leftover favors that might be put to some future use. Because these items are stored in one place, and only pulled out for parties, you'll always have a good supply on hand. One less detail to plan!

If you aren't independently wealthy and would like to stock your party closet nonetheless, scour local second-hand stores for dishes, glassware, and flatware. Keep one element the same—color, style, or pattern—and your guests will think of you as eclectic, rather than dirt-poor.

Whether you're using matched china or thrift-store finds, always make sure your party tools are clean, polished, and in good repair. Everything looks better when sparkling!

Planning Party Entertainment

Although you might think your menu and your sparkling personality are enough amusement or *any* party, you might want to consider adding some entertainment into the mix. Whether it be music, activities, or professional entertainment, your guests will have a great time if the entertainment is presented with the right attitude—fun!

tip

Take a cue from moderately priced restaurants and make "rollups" several days before your party. Nestle a complete set of cutlery—knife, fork, and spoon—in one napkin, and roll it up. Secure the roll with clear tape (if you're using paper napkins) or some other festive touch, such as theme-related napkin holders, or tuck the end of the napkin into the roll.

caution

If you are thrift-store shopping for your party tools, avoid any plates or glasses made with lead. Generally, old china, glazed terra cotta or clay dishes, or dishes with highly decorated, multicolored interior surfaces can contain lead. If you are in doubt, err on the side of caution. Lead poisoning can lead to serious health consequences.

tip

Cloth napkins don't have to be expensive! Most housewares stores sell white cloth napkins in bulk for under $20. Invest in a couple of packages and you'll be covered for a long time. Also look for plain, matching napkins at discount and closeout stores. Starched napkins fold and retain their shape better than limp napkins, so bust out that can of spray starch and heat up the iron.

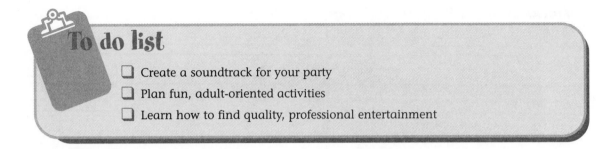

To do list

☐ Create a soundtrack for your party
☐ Plan fun, adult-oriented activities
☐ Learn how to find quality, professional entertainment

Napkin-Folding 101

Although you don't have to display napkins of which the Ritz-Carlton would approve, some basic skill with napkin folding will add an elegant touch to your table.

- **Triangle**—Fold napkin in half diagonally. Fold corners up to meet the top point. Turn napkin over and fold in half diagonally. Pick up at center and stand on base of triangle (see Figure 3.1).

FIGURE 3.1
The triangle.

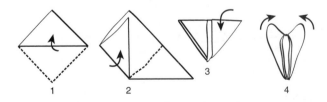

- **Glass fan**—Fold napkin in half lengthwise. Accordion pleat napkin from top to bottom. Fold bottom third of napkin back under. Place bottom in wine glass and spread out top pleats of napkin so that it resembles a fan (see Figure 3.2).

FIGURE 3.2

The glass fan.

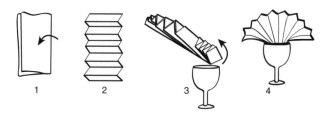

- **Standing fan**—Fold napkin in half lengthwise. Fold into $1/2$" accordion pleats, beginning at the bottom of the napkin and only pleating half the napkin. Fold the whole napkin in half, so that pleat meets pleat, with the accordion fold on the outside. Fold upper-right corner of unpleated sides diagonally down to folded base of pleats, and turn under edge, adjusting the fan until it feels stable. Place on table and spread pleats to form fan (see Figure 3.3).

FIGURE 3.3

The standing fan.

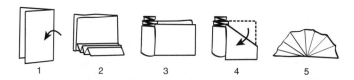

- **Tower**—Fold napkin in half diagonally. Fold corners to meet at top point. Turn napkin over and fold bottom two thirds way up. Turn napkin around and bring corners together, tucking one corner into the other. Turn napkin around and stand on base (see Figure 3.4).

FIGURE 3.4
The tower.

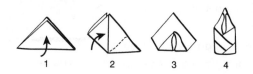

- **No-brainer**—Fold napkin in half diagonally. Holding the top point of the triangle, pull it through a round napkin holder. Attractively arrange bottom portion of napkin.

Although napkin-folding isn't for everyone, some people really enjoy the added touch of class. If you find yourself adept at linen origami, consider investing in one of the many handy books on napkin folding, which you will find in the "entertaining" section of your bookstore.

Putting Your Party to Music

Music is perhaps the single-most important ingredient to the paella that is your party. Without music, you run the risk of long, uncomfortable silences, during which your party can nose dive. A prominently displayed CD collection will also give nervous guests and wallflower types something with which to occupy themselves until the party has moved into full swing.

Music sets the atmosphere; consider carefully the soundtrack for your party. If you can, coordinate your music with your party's theme: country/western for barbecues, disco for disco parties, and swing for martini parties. Also think about the types of activities you'll feature, and coordinate your soundtrack to reflect the mood you'll want to set. For example

- For a *seated dinner*, plan a few lively CDs for pre-dinner festivities. When the guests move to the dining table, switch to mellow music—classical, vocals, or ambient house music—so you can hear conversation without shouting. Also remember to adjust the volume accordingly.

- A *casual mixer* will fare well with classic or contemporary rock, country, bluegrass, or R&B—just make sure to keep the volume loud enough to hear, but quiet enough to encourage chatter.

- If you're having a *cocktail party*, opt for smooth jazz, swingy '60s vocals (Peggy Lee or Frank Sinatra) or low-key house music. Again, watch the volume.

You'll want to experiment with different sounds and styles before the party. Try to achieve a mix of the standard and the unexpected. For interesting ideas, visit your local independent music store and chat up the clerks.

> **tip** Whatever your soundtrack, select your CDs *ahead* of time. You don't want to waste valuable party time fumbling with CD cases or rifling through your collection. Stack up about 10 CDs next to the player, in the order you'd like to play them. Toward the end of the party, as things wind down (or get nuts!), take requests.

After you select your party soundtrack, check each CD to ensure there aren't any scratches. Also, make sure you keep the remote in your pocket at all times, just to make certain the volume fluctuates with the party.

If you're on a budget and your CD collection reflects it, visit used CD stores, where you can find great albums at rock-bottom prices. Also considering visiting your local public library, where you will find many great CDs—free!

A CD COLLECTION THAT KNOWS HOW TO PARTY

Although your musical tastes might run to speed metal, British punk, or Broadway show tunes, your guests might prefer something a little more diverse. You can't please all your guests at once, but you *can* acquire a CD collection that will get the party grooving.

Recommended in no particular order, the following CDs can enliven even the most staid party, serving as everything from a background for conversation to a shake-your-booty enticer.

- ✳ **Pink Martini, *Sympathique*—**Fabulous standards, classical, and world music interpreted by an acid-cool jazz band and vocalist, this album's variety and scope make this CD a perfect party opener.

- ✳ **ABBA, *ABBA Gold: Greatest Hits*—**Disco, disco, and more disco! You might be tired of hearing *Dancing Queen*, but isn't there certain value in knowing all the words?

- ✳ **Massive Attack, *Blue Lines*—**The definitive trip-hop album, *Blue Lines* lends perfect atmosphere to almost any kind of party.

* **Kruder & Dorfmeister,** *The K&D Sessions*—Cool, low-key, trippy music characterizes this brilliant album by German remixers Peter Kruder and Richard Dorfmeister. Your hip guests will love this CD.

* **Seal,** *Seal* (1994)—The production value alone makes this CD a keeper, but the songs are great, too! Perfect for the first two hours of the party.

* **Sade,** *Love Deluxe*—When you've finished listening to Seal, slip on Sade, whose cool, "dancey" vocals will keep the party warm.

* **Annie Lennox,** *Bare*—Former Eurythmics chanteuse Annie Lennox has an amazing voice, showcased nicely by this collection of original songs, perfect for ambient moments.

* **Ella Fitzgerald,** *Ella Fitzgerald Sings the Cole Porter Songbook*—Nothing says "class" like the First Lady of Jazz. Ella is at her best when singing Cole Porter, whose clever lyrics will be familiar to any guests born before the year 1980.

* **Peggy Lee,** *The Best of Miss Peggy Lee*—An upbeat complement to Ella and Annie, Peggy Lee will inspire your guests to sing along as they sip martinis.

* **Various Artists,** *Bossa Nova Brasil*—What's a party without a little Bossa Nova? The cool, Latin rhythms will enhance any party, seated or standing.

* **Ry Cooder, Buena Vista Social Club,** *Buena Vista Social Club*—Cuban rhythms have become popular in the last decade; check out the album that started it all.

* **Led Zeppelin,** *Led Zeppelin II*—Your collection would be incomplete without at least one solid rock album. This is the album.

* **Steely Dan,** *A Decade Of Steely Dan*—The definitive party band of the 1970s, Steely Dan will leave guests nostalgic for the days when uninhibited drug use and casual sex were socially and medically acceptable.

* **Various Artists,** *Rock Instrumental Classics, Vol. 4*—You might think "Instrumental versions of my favorite rock music? No way!" Way. Perfect for quiet parties and seated dinners, where the original recordings might be far too disruptive and loud, this album really rocks.

* **Sly & the Family Stone,** *Anthology*—Sly gives disco a little soul, as evidenced by this classic collection that contains some of the best dancing songs you will ever hear.

* **Sugarhill Gang,** *The Best Of Sugarhill Gang: Rapper's Delight*—Old-school rap is perfect when your guests are likely to know every single word. Slap on this CD and watch your guests sing as they groove.

* **Yo-Yo Ma,** *Bach: The Cello Suites*—When understated occasions demand classic music, Yo-Yo Ma's take on Bach can lend a poignant air of beauty to any gathering.

Although you will certainly want to amass a larger, more extensive collection of albums that reflects your personal taste—save the speed metal for *after* the guests leave—these CDs will give you a great start.

Incorporating Activities

Party games and other activities might seem passé, but really, they aren't. When presented with the proper attitude—mirth, optimism, and a tongue-in-cheek attitude—games and activities can add an element of fun to even the stuffiest gathering. You might be surprised by how many guests will demand games and activities at your next party.

Although you'll do best wandering through a game store or consulting a party activities book (yes, these do exist), keep in mind a few options that have worked well for me:

- **Adult party games**—Allowing guests to showcase their particular talents, knowledge, and skills, adult party games can bring disparate guests together into a cohesive group. Although you probably don't want to pull out the Trivial Pursuit game for a party of 40 people, smaller gatherings are perfectly suited for an hour or two of challenging mind games. See the sidebar for specific ideas about which games work well.

- **Scavenger hunts**—This childhood favorite can become a favorite with adults when given a mature spin. At the beginning of a destination party, hand the guests a list of items (perhaps a few naughty items?) they should be able to locate throughout the evening. You also can host a video or musical scavenger hunt, or plan an entire party around a city-wide scavenger hunt.

- **Shower games**—Although some guests will claim to abhor the silly little games played at wedding and baby showers, I adore them. Keep it simple, no more than two or three games per party, and offer fun prizes. If you adopt a festive spirit, your guests will, too.

Although some gatherings, such as a Games Night, demand certain activities, games should never be forced on anyone. Take your party's temperature before pulling out the Pictionary game: If everyone is having a great time already, leave well enough alone. If your guests seem to be looking for something to do, suggest an activity or game.

Before your party, make sure all your boxed games contain all the pieces and that any tools you'll need are on hand.

tip Please offer prizes for winners! Although selecting and wrapping these small gifts might seem like one extra chore, prizes make the games even more fun, giving guests something to vie for. The prizes don't have to be expensive—scented candles, a CD or DVD, or a funky coffee mug—but they should reflect some thought. Don't forget to remove the price tags!

If you can't afford a bunch of adult games—most cost around $25—don't despair. Hit the kids section of your local Target or Wal-Mart and select a few lower-priced options, such as Uno, Yahtzee, or Operation. Look for games that allow several players, and don't forget to hype up the kitsch value!

PARTY GAMES

If you and your guests love charades, have at it. Otherwise, you might want to check out one of these other games, all suitable for adults:

* **Pictionary**—Whether you make your own set or buy the game, Pictionary is a great group game just about anyone can play.

* **Twister**—Yes, it's kitschy, but isn't that the point?

* **Taboo**—This cheeky game is a great ice-breaker for adults who think they know one another. Don't take the game too seriously, and you'll have a great time.

* **Hide-and-seek**—Best played outdoors, in a park or while camping, hide-and-seek, when played with adults (especially those who have been drinking just a little bit), can be just as fun as it was when you were a kid.

* **Trivial Pursuit**—It's a classic, with good reason. Playing in teams allows to you match skills and knowledge, and players can have a great time arguing about their final answers.

* **"I Never"**—This sorority-days holdover is actually quite fun in the right company. A drinking game, one person states something they profess never to have done, such as making out in public, and whoever has actually performed this feat takes a drink. Yes, this isn't a very mature game, but if begun at the right time, with the right group of people, you'll have a fabulous time.

* **Cranium**—Another game marketed for adults, Cranium contains a little bit for everyone: trivia, acting skills, drawing, and modeling with clay. Best suited for smaller gatherings, Cranium is one of the more fun games to emerge in recent years.

Keep a variety of games on hand, perhaps a book on party games, and you'll be able to enliven a party that is dying prematurely.

Hiring Entertainment

If you have the inclination, consider hiring professional entertainment for your party. Although not every gathering—or budget!—is suited to this type of activity, a little creativity and effort on your part can make your evening's entertainment spectacular.

Instead of hiring your brother's garage band, why not explore one of these ideas?

- **Music**—Quality performers are always welcome at any party, especially when they function more as ambience, rather than the central focus. Consider a string quartet, jazz trio, or even a harpist, all of whom can add wonderful atmosphere to your gathering without overpowering it.

  If you're working with a limited budget, but are dying for professional musicians at your party, contact a local university or music school, where you can often find talented students who are more than happy to play for the exposure and a small fee.

- **Live entertainment**—A hypnotist, comedian, or balloon artist can add a lively, silly element to the right party, such as a barbecue, retirement or reunion party, children's party, or picnic. Before you dismiss this idea as childish, think about it: What could be more entertaining than a group of adults laughing their heads off at a professional clown?

- **Services**—A really creative hostess will have fun planning special services for the right party: a psychic, a tarot card reader, or a palm-reader for a Halloween party; an esthetician for a Beauty Night; a 5-minute masseuse for a Happy Hour; or even a babysitter for a party at which several children will be present. Think about the theme of your party and your guests' needs and preferences, and then look through your local community paper to discover what kinds of services are available near you.

Although not every party will require or benefit from hired entertainment—a dinner party for six might be an odd place for a babysitter—many parties can be enhanced by such offerings. Be creative and ask your friends for feedback. You might be surprised by what you hear!

If you have the budget for a professional entertainer or service provider, don't skimp on quality. Ask for references, attend an event at which the person will be performing, and make sure you are getting your money's worth.

> **tip** Always keep your guests' happiness in mind. Not everyone will appreciate a comedian who tells off-color jokes or a performance by a psychic or fortuneteller, which many people negatively associate with the occult. If your guests are on the conservative side, plan accordingly.

Give yourself plenty of time to research, evaluate, and select your entertainment. Because this is one task you can definitely perform far ahead of your party date, don't leave it to the last minute, or else you might find yourself settling for second-rate talent.

Offering Party Favors

Although not absolutely essential to the success of your party, small favors are a nice way of thanking your guests for attending your party. Because many people will bring wine, food, or hostess gifts, it's a gracious touch to offer something in return.

Try not to waste your money on stupid favors. If you're going low-budget, make sure the item will be perceived as kitschy, not tacky. If you have a budget that will accommodate elegance, make sure your favors are useful and interesting. There is no point in spending money and time on favors that will be thrown away when the guest gets home.

Party favors should be inexpensive and specific to your party's theme or occasion. Although almost any small, interesting memento will suffice, here are a few suggestions for favors that work:

- Bulk-printed matchbooks with your name and the date of your event—although this concept is a standard for wedding receptions and other largescale events, consider these favors for smaller parties, as well. Your guests will find printed matchbooks a surprising favor at a cocktail party, and the cost is less than you might imagine.
- Polaroid pictures taken at the event, and then slipped into preprinted cards; guests pick up the cards on their way out the door.
- Miniature bottles of champagne or airplane-sized liquor (about $2 each), decorated with theme-specific trimming.
- For Girly Parties, little makeup bags filled with hair accessories, inexpensive cosmetics, or nail polish.
- Small boxes of incense (about $2 each), tied with an inexpensive burner (as little as $1).
- For an outdoor or garden party, individual seed packets or flower bulbs wrapped in cheesecloth, with instructions for growing attached.

If your budget does not allow for much money to spend on favors, think *way* outside the box. Shop at Mexican or Chinese variety stores and look for kitschy little items for as little as a quarter.

Creativity counts when it comes to favors, so get those juices flowing and shop closeout stores for unique trinkets. Favors also serve as a memento of your party, reminding guests what a fabulous time they had at your event and possibly prompting them to plan something of their own.

Summary

Now that you are familiar with the basics involved with throwing a party—theme, décor, food and drink, entertainment, and favors—it's time to put that information to use by planning your very own party. But wait! Before you progress to Part II, you still have one bit of education left: manners. In the next chapter, you will learn some basic rules of social etiquette, including how to behave at the table, how to handle difficult situations, and what is expected of you as the host.

tip

At my wedding, we gave out homemade mixed CDs with songs featured at our reception. After I compiled the playlist, a friend downloaded the songs (free!) and burned them onto a CD. We purchased bulk packages of CDs and inexpensive plastic cases, burned enough copies for each of our guests, and printed out liner notes for very little cost. Many guests said these were the best favors they ever received—and we only spent about $50.

Minding Your Ps and Qs

An essential component for hosting a successful party, old-fashioned good manners are far from obsolete. Just because few of us bother to learn them any more, it doesn't mean they aren't worth learning!

Don't despair; I'm not going to insist you become Emily Post's doppelganger. We don't have nearly enough time together for such a transformation! Instead, I'm going to lay down a few rules for learning and applying etiquette for everyday party situations, including

- Guest list dos, don'ts, and do-at-your-own-risks
- Guidelines for the well-mannered host
- Table and serving manners
- Ways to deal with party fouls
- Ending the party with grace and tact

You don't have to be perfect. Your guests will still love you even if you serve red wine with fish. In this chapter, I am far more concerned with making sure you don't *drop* the fish on your guests—and showing you what to do if it happens.

Putting Together a Guest List

Compiling the guest list can be tricky. You want to create a good mix of people, and yet you don't want to offend anyone by excluding them. You want to ensure you have a lively group, and yet you want to avoid potential catastrophes at all costs. What's a host to do? Read on!

Mixing Groups

Parties are a wonderful way to introduce friends to one another, be it a romantic fix up or two people who both love Boston terriers. Potential mixed groups might include

- Book group and writing group members
- Dog-park friends and neighborhood friends
- Your significant other's friends and your friends
- People from different departments at work or school
- Members from both sides of the family
- Friends from college and friends from high school

Use common sense to decide which groups to mix, and then go from there. Do you work in a stuffy academic environment? Perhaps your co-workers might not enjoy meeting your metal-head college friends. Is everyone in your book group "allergic" to dogs? Perhaps they might not appreciate your dog-park friends. You really never know who is going to hit it off—all you can do is combine "ingredients" that seem like they will go together and hope your chemistry with both groups is enough to stimulate lively conversation.

tip Keep numbers in mind when you're considering which friends to invite. If you want to invite 30 work friends and your significant other wants to invite another 30 people, and you are planning a barbecue party for 40, either select two different groups or change the kind of party you give.

You can always use money as an excuse to invite only a few people from each group. Just make sure you send invitations to your selected guests at home, not at work, with a note saying that you're only having a small gathering and can't quite manage inviting the whole office this time. Your invited guests will understand that they should keep quiet about the party. If word does get out that you're having a party, you can always save face by telling people you're having a small party, but you can't afford to invite the whole group this time. People might grumble, but they will understand.

A WORD OF CAUTION

When you are considering inviting just a few individuals from among a small group of your co-workers or associates, be very careful. In most cases, you save yourself and others unnecessary embarrassment if you include everyone in the group.

For example, if you work closely with a group of four volunteers, don't invite Sean and Leslie and neglect Melanie and Rachel. Likewise, if you want to invite four out of the five people from your department at work, you'd better invite the fifth person, too. In both cases, you will leave the uninvited members of the group feeling left out and insulted. And, inevitably, those you have invited will find themselves in an awkward situation when they discuss the invitation or the event in front of the uninvited co-worker.

Although you might think that word won't get back to Melanie, Rachel, or that sad sack who sits by the Xerox machine, you are very wrong. People love to talk, especially about things other than work. Save yourself a headache and make an inclusive guest list.

Of course, you don't have to invite everyone you work with or everyone who volunteers at the shelter, only those with whom you come into direct contact on a regular basis; this note of caution is only applicable for the smaller groups of friends, especially if the people in the group know one another well and talk frequently.

Inviting People Who Hate One Another

At one memorable party my then-roommate and I gave in our early twenties, I had personal experience with what happens when you invite two people who hate one another to the same event.

Two friends in our circle had just broken up, quite unpleasantly. Because my roommate and I were young and relatively inexperienced with matters of etiquette, we didn't think to confer with one another about the guest list. I invited one half of the broken-up couple, and my roommate invited the other.

Although both guests promised to behave like mature adults, one of them eventually had too much to drink, lost her temper, and threw the entire contents of her very large drink glass at her former boyfriend, drenching several innocent bystanders.

Here is the valuable lesson I learned: Do not invite two people who hate one another to the same party, especially if either of them is likely to make a scene. Yes, it will be difficult to choose which of your friends to invite to your gathering, but if you strongly suspect that your friends might make a ruckus, then you have every right to choose between them. Try to stagger your invites: Cindy gets to come to one party, and Ken gets to come to the next.

If you feel as though the two guests will really behave themselves, and you are hosting an important occasion, such as a wedding, funeral, or baby shower, let both guests know the other will be attending and tell them you hope this won't cause any discomfort for either of them at the event. If the bad feelings are still running high, gracefully accept the fact that one—or both—of them may opt out.

If you have any friends who are recovering alcoholics, and you are planning a martini party, let those guests know that alcohol will be a central component to the party. Be kind and understanding, but not patronizing, and let them know that although you would love for them to come, you will understand completely if they prefer not to wallow in a boozy environment.

DON'T BE TACKY

Although you might be tempted to throw a theme party when someone reaches a particular life milestone—such as the Big Four-Oh—there is no need to be tacky about it. Even if the guest of honor is approaching his Big Day with humor and self-deprecating jokes, don't pile it on at the party, featuring toupee samples, adult diapers, and prune juice. Although the birthday boy might smile politely and attempt a laugh at his own expense, chances are good that he might be crying inside. Unless the 40-year-old throws his own "Over the Hill" party—or insists you do it for him—celebrate his birthday as you would any other year.

Likewise, before you throw your co-worker a huge surprise party, make sure she will appreciate it. Surprise parties certainly aren't for everyone; many people cringe at the thought of being shouted at by a bunch of people lurking in the darkness. To avoid spoiling the potential surprise, you might relay a manufactured anecdote about a surprise party given for you, and note your co-worker's reaction. If you see horror on her face, change the surprise to a planned event.

Being a Good Host

Although as the host you have many responsibilities, you only have one primary goal: to ensure your guests have a fabulous time at your party. However, realizing this goal means you'll need to perform a number of duties as a host.

Providing a Clean, Safe Environment

Before the party starts, take a long, honest look around you. Does your home or apartment look like you hosted a frat party the night before? If so, you have no business hosting a gathering until you clean up the mess. Have a garage sale, buy a book on home-keeping, or consult a professional organizer.

Sort through the detritus that clutters your home, and ask yourself, "Do I love this thing? Does looking at it make me happy?" If both answers are anything but "Yes!" then ditch it. Find a home for everything else that remains. Shutting doors and shoving piles under the bed is cheating; some busybody *will* find you out, so take a day and get rid of the clutter—forever.

After your home is organized, ready it from top to bottom, including

- Removing trash, weeds, and pet "deposits" from outside areas
- Thoroughly cleaning the bathroom and kitchen, as well as any other rooms into which guests might wander
- Vacuuming, sweeping, and/or mopping the floors
- Stocking up on toilet paper, facial tissue, and paper towels
- Removing or stashing in a safe anything dangerous, such as firearms or drugs, including prescription drugs
- Fixing potentially harmful situations, such as broken glass or missing steps
- Ensuring guests will have adequate lighting around any "dangerous" areas, such as your driveway or yard

If you are expecting children at your party, take a few precautions: Install a package or two of inexpensive child-safety devices for any low-to-the-ground electrical outlets and any cabinets containing poisons or household cleaners. Although it is not your responsibility to monitor the safety of your guests' children, the parents will certainly appreciate your kind gesture.

> **tip**
>
> "A place for everything and everything in its place" is an excellent axiom by which to live. Find a place for everything in your home: mail, paperwork, kids' toys, dog paraphernalia, clothing, kitchen items, books, CDs, toiletries—everything. When you use something, put it back when you are done using it. The easiest way to clean up before a party is to have a house that is clutter-free.

Greeting Guests Warmly

As the host, you are expected to greet each guest that comes through your door for the first hour of the party. Because many people still believe that it is rude to arrive late, be prepared for your doorbell to ring up to 30 minutes before your party is scheduled to begin. The food and beverages should be ready to go; you and your housemate(s) should be showered, dressed, and smiling; and your home should be clean and ready to receive guests.

As each person arrives, do the following:

- Open the door with a smile on your face.
- Make sure you know the guests' names: "Hi, you must be [insert name of housemate]'s friends. I don't think we've met?" You will need this information later in the party, when you are introducing these guests to other people. Try to create an instant mnemonic device for remembering names: "Patty's Purse is Pink" or something equally silly and memorable.
- Ask to take coats and bags, or direct guests to an appropriate spot to stash their things, such as a bed in a room with a closed door.
- Escort your guests to the food or beverage table, or ensure they have a place to roost.

By taking a few moments with each guest, you will begin the event with everyone feeling welcomed and appreciated.

For latecomers, don't stress too much about answering the door if you are busy with other important tasks, such as basting the turkey. Let someone else answer the door, but make sure you appear within a few minutes to say hello.

Making Introductions

Although introducing people by telling them thoughtful, interesting details about one another might not have worked well for Bridget Jones, it's still the best way to make an introduction.

For example, when introducing people who otherwise have nothing in common, you might say, "John, this is Alicia, my friend from book group; Alicia, this is John, my husband's best friend from college. You both have incredibly cute dogs!"

The aforementioned example provided three important details:

1. Both people's names, spoken twice each
2. A frame of reference for how you know each of them (book group; husband's college friend)
3. An interesting fact about which they might converse

tip If you forget someone's name as you are about to make introductions, try not to stand there, visibly flummoxed, with your mouth hanging open. Instead, pretend you have just remembered something very important in the kitchen. Look startled, begin to leave, turn back to your introductees, apologize, and explain that you need to take care of something quickly. Politely ask them to introduce themselves, and promise you'll return in a moment to see how they're doing. Although slightly tacky, this move is preferable to 'fessing up that you can't remember your own guests' names.

After providing this introduction, you are now free to leave the two guests to talk among themselves.

Working the Room

Although you will certainly be occupied with any number of critical tasks (last-minute meal preparations, for example) during the party, you still need to work the room every 30 minutes or so, ensuring your guests are having a great time and don't need anything. This activity is also known as *mingling*.

If you aren't a marketing professional, working the room might seem daunting, but it really isn't. Try this plan:

- Begin at one point, like the kitchen, and work counter-clockwise, from right to left, stopping at each group of people for about two minutes.

- Wait for a break in the conversation, and then ask if everyone is having a good time or needs anything. Try to connect with each person, making her feel special, as if she is the most important person in the room.

- Monitor the conversation; if it seems to be falling flat, introduce a new topic or tell a silly joke. If someone appears to be feeling awkward (arms crossed, darting eyes, shifting his weight, and staring into the distance), relocate him to another group, saying you've been meaning to introduce him to so-and-so.

- After a moment or two, move on to the next group. A light touch on the arm or an "I'd better see how so-and-so is doing" are courteous exits.

As you wander, try to look simultaneously purposeful and open to questions. You want to seem available to your guests, but you don't want to get too caught up in a particular conversation until you have finished working the room.

Also, subtlety is the key to successful mingling. You don't want to force your way into conversations, breaking up party momentum with an inopportune inquiry as to guests' happiness. Unobtrusively working the room is all about timing; make sure you take the pulse of each conversing group before getting involved.

tip If you notice any stranded guests, men or women who are alone and look as though they are not enjoying their solitary status, mosey over and try to feel them out: Are they happy sitting alone? Move on. Do they seem a little nervous, shy, or otherwise unhappy? Introduce them to someone whose company they might enjoy, or enlist their help with a fun, simple task, such as changing the CD or helping out with the appetizers. Be tactful, and don't make them feel like a loser or an indentured servant; chances are good that they will embrace the opportunity to do something useful.

Keep mingling until the food or main event is ready. When the dinner or entertainment is over, begin mingling again. As the evening winds to a close, you can spend more time with particular guests, but you should still keep an eye out for anyone who looks like they might need a host's graceful touch.

Using (and Encouraging) Proper Table Manners

The host really only has one hard-and-fast rule when it comes to table manners: The host does not begin eating until all the guests are served; likewise, the guests do not begin eating until the host has taken the first bite. That said, both guests and host make any party nicer by following a number of basic rules of table etiquette.

Leading by Example

There is really no graceful way to correct a guest's manners, no matter how inappropriate they might seem. The best way to ensure your guests behave nicely is to set a good example. Practice these rules of good manners on a daily basis, and you won't need to learn them in time for your next party:

- Don't bring anything extra to the table: chewing gum, tobacco, cigarettes, cocktail glasses, or uneaten bits of finger food.
- When you sit down, place your napkin in your lap and leave it there. If you need to step into another room, leave your napkin on your chair and replace it on your lap when you return. When you have finished eating and are ready to leave the table, place your napkin next to your plate.
- Don't season your food until you have first tasted it. Automatically dumping salt or ketchup onto your meal is insulting to the person who prepared it. If, after tasting, you would prefer more salt or pepper, flavor away.
- Don't saw up all your meat at once; cut no more than two pieces at a time, resting your knife on the edge of your plate as you eat each bite.
- Do not make food-related noises while eating. This means no gurgling, swishing, slurping, or "yummy" noises. Along these lines, do not chew with your mouth open or talk with food in your mouth.
- Do not rest your elbows on the table, pick food out from between your teeth, wash down your food with a beverage, burp, fart, or do anything else you would not do in front of your mother.

- If you need to remove something from your mouth (olive pit, gristle), place it directly on the edge of your plate, using your napkin to camouflage the act, if possible. Don't spit the offending bit into your napkin; raise your fork to your mouth, slide the unwanted inedible back onto your fork, and then return it to your plate.

- If you need to cough or sneeze, turn your head away from the table and cover your face with your hand.

- Do not eat your food as if wild boars are after you. Take your time, and enjoy the food you prepared.

- Don't rush your guests. Allow them all the time they need to enjoy the meal, and encourage conversation.

- Accidents happen. If someone spills something, even if it's on your grand-mother's prized linen tablecloth, react with aplomb, assuring your guest that there isn't any problem, and quickly fetch whatever you need to clean up the spill.

Don't be too nervous about table manners; you don't want to become so caught up in minding your Ps and Qs that you become a frazzled mess. Try your best to be polite and genteel, and hope your guests follow your good example. Remain focused on your real goal: providing an atmosphere in which guests can relax, enjoy them-selves, and eat the wonderful food you've prepared.

Making Dinner Conversation

As you and your guests enjoy the meal, practice the same skills you used while working the room: Monitor conversations, forestall silences, make sure everyone has everything they need, and try to be proactive about potential disasters.

If you find that conversation is lagging, don't be overly concerned. Chances are good that your guests are simply relishing their food. However, if the silence becomes oppressive, it's up to you, the host, to break it with a little dinner conversation.

You might feel nervous, but don't let it show. Project an image of confidence and relaxation, and your guests will follow suit. If you're stumped for openers, try a few of these suggestions:

- If a guest has had a reason to celebrate recently (promotion at work, addition to the family, an award or recognition), share the good news, assuming it is something the relevant parties would enjoy discussing: "So, Sean, are you and Erin excited about your pending adoption?" or "Carl, I hear you've been promoted to a new position at work."

- Books, music, and movies are always good conversation fodder: "So, I just saw the *The Notebook*…they did a great job of adapting the book to film, didn't they?"
- If you've heard an interesting news item that is suitable for dinner conversation (nothing gory, volatile, or related to politics), bring up the topic for discussion: "Did you guys hear about the new study on dolphin intelligence?"
- You can also discuss happenings in your own life, assuming they are appropriate for dinner conversation: "Rob and I are thinking about going to Kauai next summer. Has anyone been there?"

Do not discuss gossip, politics, or religion—topics that are certain to begin a debate. Likewise, don't bring up anything too personal or a happening that might not yet have been announced ("So, Doug, I hear you and Shannon are trying to conceive!").

If your guests stray into forbidden territory, gently guide them to safer subjects at the first opportune moment. Don't abruptly change the subject ("So, how about those Lakers?"), which will only make your guests uncomfortable. Merely steer the conversation to something less volatile. Above all, try to enjoy yourself. This might be the only time you get to sit down all night.

When Disaster Strikes

Part of ensuring your guests have a fabulous time is making sure disaster *doesn't* strike. You may experience guests engaging in rude behaviors, such as smoking in an off-limits room, bringing uninvited guests, or behaving in an inappropriate manner.

Although every hostess hopes for a flawless party, faux pas do and will happen. As the hostess, it is up to you to respond to these party fouls with grace. Use equal parts of common sense, tact, and humor to defuse potentially perilous situations, and you'll be fine.

Try to keep your eyes open and your wits about you throughout the event—that means you can't drink too much or make yourself otherwise incapable of spotting conflict or problems before they arise.

Letting Your Guests Know the House Rules

People usually try to do what is expected of them, especially in social situations; the trick is setting reasonable expectations in a way that doesn't make you appear (or feel) uptight or micro-managerial.

A NOTE ABOUT SERVING

As the hostess, it is your responsibility to serve the food, especially if you are hosting a sit-down meal. Although no one will expect professional table service from you, you can certainly observe a few rules of etiquette.

* To serve while standing (salads, desserts, and coffee), serve the guest to the right of your place at the table, working your way around until you return to your own seat. Serve yourself a portion, set the dish on the table, and return to the kitchen for the next dish, if applicable. Serve from the left; clear from the right. Do not take a plate until a guest has finished with it.

* To serve a full dinner, place all the dishes on the table before calling in the guests. You may leave the meat or main course for last, if you wish to make a presentation of it.

* To serve from the table, place a small amount of food on your plate and pass the dish to the right. When it has made a complete round of the table, you may take another serving.

If you are hosting a buffet, your main task is to ensure the dishes remain full. If you have additional portions, refill the dishes as soon as they are three-fourths empty. If you do not have additional food, wait until the dishes are completely empty, and then remove them to the kitchen.

Unless it is absolutely necessary, try to place all serving dishes on the table before beginning the meal. Although it is lovely to play "five-star waiter," you will be tired enough from the preparation and mingling. Let guests serve themselves, especially during the main course.

Before your party, decide on a few house rules:

* Do you permit smoking in the house? If so, set out several ashtrays in each room. If you want to limit smoking to particular rooms, only set ashtrays in those rooms and close the doors to any areas where smoking is not allowed. If you don't want anyone to smoke in the house, try to let guests know *before* they light up, if only to save them embarrassment.

* Will pets or children be allowed to attend? If not, inform your guests ahead of time.

* Are guests allowed to bring additional people? Either way, let guests know ahead of time.

* Will guests think they should bring a gift? Although many guests will bring a hostess gift, many will not think of it. Never chastise someone for failing to bring a gift; instead, thank those who do and try to unwrap it immediately.

- Will there be alcohol served at the party? If you are hosting a sober celebration, be sure to let guests know this ahead of time. Although a polite guest will not turn down a sober invitation, she will want to know that she should not bring wine or spirits as a gift for you.

After you have determined which rules will govern your party, gently inform guests of your expectations and help them to meet them—or bypass them, if necessary—in a manner that makes them feel special, not a huge pain in the rear.

The best way to inform guests about your house rules is to let your invitations do the talking for you. For birthdays, anniversaries, showers, and other occasions on which gifts are traditionally given, think ahead. Would you prefer guests not bring gifts? If so, announce your preference on the invitations: "No gifts, please." If you would prefer for children or pets not to attend, a polite "adults only" or "no pets, please" will suffice. The same holds true for alcohol, if you would prefer to omit it from your party. If you have restrictions about smoking, print up a few "no smoking, please" signs and place them in unobtrusive, but easily spotted, locations (the bathroom, near the buffet table, or bar).

Handling Uninvited Guests

If one of your invited guests shows up with a friend (or five) in tow, do your best to make each guest, invited or uninvited, feel comfortable and welcome. No excited exclamations, "But this is a formal dinner party for six! Do you expect me to pull another pound of meat from behind my ear?" Stay calm until your guests are ensconced, and then retire to a bathroom or closet to vent your frustration on a pillow—or your significant other.

If the uninvited guests prove a real problem—such as in the case of the aforementioned formal dinner—deal with it. Send a friend to the store for more food or booze. Unobtrusively set another plate. Raid the house for additional seating. Quickly make out another place card. Chances are good that you will be able to accommodate another guest quite easily, so try not to blow the issue out of proportion. Really, the more the merrier. If the invited guest has displayed truly heinous judgment in bringing his posse, have a word with him *after* the party.

Putting a Stop to Rudeness

There is never any reason for rudeness, from anyone, *ever*. If you see a guest behaving rudely, take immediate and tactful action. If you hear about such behavior from another guest, try to observe the behavior for yourself before saying a word.

After you have determined the guest is out of line, ask her to help you with something in the kitchen. When you are alone, out of earshot of other guests, engage the guest in conversation about her behavior. Try to ask a gentle, opening question ("So, how are you feeling today, Trisha?") and listen carefully. If the guest is having a personal problem or is simply having a bad day, listening will do a great deal to alleviate the problem. Here are some other tips for dealing gracefully with rude behavior:

- If the rude act was unintentional, and you were in the vicinity when your guest committed it (a slightly off-color joke, a too-personal question), immediately diffuse the situation with humor and change the subject.

- If the unintentionally rude act was committed outside your presence ("Jane, you will not *believe* what Howie just said to me…"), downplay it and steer the guest toward a different conversation.

- If the rudeness is simply intolerable (starting a verbal or physical fight), tactfully suggest that it might be time to leave. If the guest refuses, enlist the help of a few discreet friends.

Dealing with rudeness is not pleasant, but it is a reality at many parties. Don't let yourself—or your party—be affected by rude behavior; always take the high road. Your guests might need to follow your lead.

Managing Smoking, Alcohol, and Drug Use

If you catch someone smoking where he has been asked to not smoke, politely ask him to move outside or to another room. You won't need to make a huge deal of his gaffe; chances are good that he simply forgot your house rule. If the person repeats the act, continue to correct him as if he has simply forgotten your house rule. Just because he is being rude does not mean you need to return the favor.

If you realize one of your guests is far too drunk for her own—or the party's—welfare, assign that person a "helper," someone who can make sure the drunkard doesn't violate anyone's personal space with rude, lewd, or obnoxious behavior. Although you might be tempted to elect yourself to this role, your primary concern is the rest of the party. Assign a housemate, your significant other, or a very good friend to the task, and thank that person later.

Unwanted drug use is a different story. Although many people are open to recreational drug use, many more are not. No matter which category best describes you, your guests should respect your choice. If you have invited a guest you know to be a habitual drug user, and you would prefer he not do drugs in your house, tell him ahead of time, in simple terms ("Hey, Jerry, leave the crystal at home, okay?").

When Jerry arrives, do not grill him about the contents of his fanny pack; trust that he has respected your wishes until he proves otherwise.

If you catch someone in the act of doing drugs, try to handle the situation with diplomacy. Although it might be difficult to remain calm if you find someone firing up a crack pipe in your bathroom, you *can* do it. Simply ask the person to refrain while in your house; if they refuse, ask an intimidating-looking friend to please escort the offending guest out the front door.

If you catch a guest *after* she has taken drugs or had too much to drink, you cannot safely allow that guest to drive away until several hours have passed, depending upon the drug. You do not want to compound your guest's inappropriate behavior by tossing her out and risking an accident—or worse. If possible, have a friend drive her home; if not, relocate her to a closed-off portion of the house, where she can cause fewer disruptions as she sobers up.

Finding Love in Unexpected Places

Although this situation seldom arises after you and your guests have graduated from college, it is still possible for you to walk in on two (or more!) guests *en fla-grante*. Unless you are hosting an orgy—a whole different book!—this behavior is unacceptable, especially if it is before midnight.

Don't make the situation worse by overreacting. Yes, your guests might have held off until the party was over. Yes, you might have preferred they chose somewhere beside your bed to consummate their passion. Regardless, you must handle things with grace and tact, just as you would any other unpleasant situation. Chances are good that your accidental discovery will prompt the lovebirds to put their clothes back on. If not, a sharp tap on the door a few minutes later should remind them to get moving. If even that fails, open the door, remaining outside, and firmly ask them to rejoin the party.

If you happen to discover a someone engaging in an inappropriate act with some-one clearly off-limits—someone else's husband or girlfriend, for example—take the same action you would if it were anyone engaged in lewd behavior (rap on the door, with a firm request to get moving). Say nothing to anyone until *after* the party. At that point, let your conscience dictate your behavior.

Closing Down Shop

All parties must end, even yours. Whether it's 3:00 p.m. or 3:00 a.m., your trickiest party task might be getting your guests to leave.

Coffee—Nature's Miracle Worker

Aside from dropping hints about an early tee time or some other equally transparent excuse, there is one sure-fire way to end the party: Brew a nice, big pot of coffee. Most adults have been conditioned to recognize coffee as the denouement to the evening's festivities. The aroma will spread throughout the house, alerting even coffee-eschewers that the time has come for this good thing to end.

Instead of carrying out cups and accoutrements for each guest, create a small coffee bar, either in the kitchen or at the bar area. Set out a pot of regular and a pot of decaff, cups or mugs, sugar, cream, spoons, and perhaps a few goodies, such as cinnamon or powdered chocolate. Announcing "Coffee's ready!" will serve as an additional reminder that things should be winding down.

Dealing with Stragglers

If serving coffee doesn't work, employ a few tricks used by barkeeps across the nation: Turn up the lights and turn down the volume. Don't be obnoxious—no one needs a spotlight shining in her face; don't be too subtle, either, lest your warnings go unheeded. A few lights turned on where once there was darkness (or dimness) is effective, as is replacing blaring house music with something a bit more ambient.

What you are not allowed to do, however, is begin cleaning up. Aside from collecting any offending trash and relocating the empty bottles to the kitchen or recycling bin, you should only begin cleaning up after the last guest leaves. If other guests try to help out, offer an obligatory admonition ("Really, Michelle, you don't have to do that…"), and then let them do all the cleaning up they please. Perhaps your stragglers will take the hint and either join in or bail out.

Yes, you need to recycle. If you anticipate a large quantity of empty bottles and cans, set out a separate trash can, with liner, and a small sign indicating that guests can toss their recyclables here. Remember to check the can throughout the party, replacing the liner bag as necessary.

A smart host will indicate the party's hours on the invitations: "8:00 p.m. 'til Midnight." If you truly do not care when the party ends, a cheery "8:00 p.m. 'til ???" will convey this information to your guests. However, be prepared for them to take you at your word!

THE DESIGNATED DRIVER

Dealing with drunken guests is an absolute reality. You *cannot* allow someone who is drunk to drive.

Although a courteous host does not demand a blood-alcohol test prior to her guests' departure, you can use your powers of observation to ensure your guests are all sober enough to drive.

According to the U.S. Departments of Health and Human Services National Institutes of Health, a Blood Alcohol Content (BAC) of .08% is considered legally intoxicated in most states. Without going into a lot of detail about body weight, rate of absorption, and elimination over time, you can use the following chart to help you determine if your guest is fit to operate a vehicle.

Drinks Consumed	Amount of Time for Sobering Up		
	Small Guest (< 120 lbs.)	Medium Guest (120–180 lbs.)	Large Guest (> 180 lbs.)
1	1 hour	1 hour	1 hour
2	2 hours	1 hour	1 hour
3	2 hours	2 hours	1 hour
4	3 hours	2 hours	2 hours
5	3 hours	3 hours	2 hours

This table is in no way meant to be legal or medical advice, but only a guide for you, as the host, to evaluate whether or not someone should be driving. If you suspect a guest is too intoxicated to drive, regardless of his size or the number of drinks he has consumed, you should always err on the side of caution and insist the person catch a ride or a cab home.

If you expect there will be a lot of drinking at your party, collect your guests' keys as they arrive at the party. Make a game of it, designating a trustworthy and sober friend to act as Keymaster (remember the movie *Say Anything*?), collecting keys from everyone and only returning them when the guest is sober enough to drive.

Thanking Your Guests

Although a good hostess will know to thank each departing guest as she shows them out the door, you might not realize that a few special thank-yous are required. Single out these acts of kindness for follow-up within the next few days of your party:

- Anyone who brought you a hostess gift other than a bottle of wine or a contribution to the buffet table
- Your Keymaster or anyone you asked to baby-sit an overly intoxicated guest, including any drivers *you* designated
- Anyone who helped you set up or break down the party, arriving early or staying late
- Anyone who did anything really special for you, such as going home to grab extra chairs for uninvited guests or rushing to the store, spending their own money on party supplies, and refusing reimbursement

You don't have to be extravagant with your thanks—a phone call or email will suffice. However, if you enjoy sending out thank-you cards, go for it! Good mail is always a pleasure to receive.

Summary

In this chapter, you learned how to be a gracious host, providing for your guests' needs and happiness above all else. I showed you the importance of creating a guest list comprised of people who, instead of wanting to start a fistfight, might want to start a friendship. You learned the core duties of a well-mannered host: providing a clean, safe environment for your guests; greeting each guest and introducing him to others; ensuring your guests are comfortable and happy; and taking time to talk to each guest individually. In addition to basic table manners, you learned how to handle difficult situations, including violations of house rules, uninvited guests, rudeness, smoking, drug use, over-the-top drinking, and inappropriate behavior. You learned how to say goodbye to your guests and how to tactfully encourage them to head home. You also learned the importance of thanking your guests, especially for behavior that went above the call of duty.

This brings us to the end of Part I, "Know Your Party Self." In Part II, "The Perfect Party," you will learn how to plan and execute the very best party for you, beginning with Chapter 5, "Planning Ahead," which will outline everything you need to do ahead of your Big Day.

Part II

The Perfect Party

Planning Ahead

5

In the next few chapters, we'll look in great detail at everything that goes into planning and hosting a party, from beginning to end. I'll plan a sample party, showing you everything that goes into it: planning the party (this chapter), getting everything ready (Chapter 6, "Counting Down"), hosting the party (Chapter 7, "The Big Day: Successfully Hosting a Party"), and cleaning up (Chapter 8, "The After Party").

In Part II, "The Perfect Party," I'll apply everything I discussed in Part I, "Know Your Party Self;" in Part III, "Variations on a Theme," I'll give you outlines for planning a wide variety of different parties, including holiday parties, occasion parties, meal parties, and theme parties. You will use the example in this chapter to create the parties in Part III, so read carefully!

In this chapter, you will learn how to plan a successful party. You learn how to set a party budget, select a date and theme, determine where you want to hold the party, compile a guest list, and choose invitations. Then, you'll plan your food and drink offerings, decide how to decorate for the party, and plan for games or other activities. You also learn about pulling together a music play list to provide the soundtrack for your party. Finally, you discover how to find or create party favors that will please your guests *and* fit your budget.

We have a lot to cover in this chapter, so grab a drink, relax, and get ready to plan a party!

In this chapter:

* Calculate a party budget
* Select the right date
* Decide on a theme
* Select the party venue
* Compile the guest list
* Decide what kinds of invitations to send out
* Plan food and drink menus and make a shopping list
* Choose a party décor
* Decide on entertainment or activities
* Select a music play list
* Find creative, inexpensive party favors
* Create a master budget, a shopping list, and a list of other things that you'll need for the party

You'll Need

☐ Notebook
☐ Calculator
☐ Pen or pencil

Planning a Party Budget

In Appendix B, "Party Tools," I've included a copy of the chart you see here. This chart will help you plan each party element to the last penny. As we plan our sample party, I will refer to this chart each time we discuss an element or a cost.

Here's the chart:

Element	Cost
Total Budget	
Invitations	
Venue	
Food	
Drink	
Tools	
Décor	
Entertainment/Activities	
Music	
Favors	
Emergency Fund	
Total Costs	

Before we get started with filling in the chart, here's a brief overview of the different element categories:

- **Total Budget**—Before you begin, you need to decide exactly how much money you have available to spend on this party. *Don't bankrupt yourself.* Pick a number, and stick with it.
- **Invitations**—If you're springing for actual paper invitations, remember to budget enough money for postage.

- **Venue**—If you're renting a venue, include the rental cost, plus any additional fees you might incur, such as a tip for the caterer or bartender. If you are giving the party at home, remember to include any furniture or equipment you'll need to rent, as well as any money you plan to spend on cleaning or gardening before the event.

- **Food**—After you decide which recipes to use, make a complete list of ingredients for your shopping list.

- **Drink**—In addition to spirits, soda, water, and ice, remember to think about mixers and garnishes.

- **Tools**—Although you might have everything you need already in your home, you might have to rent or purchase a grill, additional seating, or tools for serving the food, such as plates, napkins, cutlery, or cups. If you're planning an outdoor party, also think about lighting.

- **Décor**—Unless you are having a theme party, your décor cost will be minimal. However, don't forget to include candles, firewood, or anything else you'll need for creating ambience.

- **Entertainment or Activities**—Include fees for any professional entertainers you'll hire or the cost of any games or activities you plan.

- **Music**—Although you probably already have enough CDs for the event, you might choose to rent a sound system, hire a DJ, or beef up your music collection.

- **Favors**—Think "cheap," and you'll only have to budget about $1 per person for favors.

- **Emergency Fund**—Before you create your budget sheet, set aside 10% of your total budget to cover emergencies.

- **Total Costs**—This amount should not exceed the number you entered in the Total Budget line.

tip Make a small investment in a party notebook. Visit your local office supply or stationery store and select a book that appeals to you: fancy or plain, tailored or frivolous. Pick some dividers, too, and label them with categories: Food, Drink, Décor, Music, Favors, Entertainment, Venue, Invitations, Guest List. As you research your parties, keep track of the information you unearth, even if you don't use it for that party. When it comes time to throw your next party, refer to your party notebook and see if you can reuse or repurpose any of the information you gathered. You'll be a step ahead of yourself, before you even begin to plan.

tip If money is a concern for you, get your party budget in cash, stow it in an envelope, along with your budget sheet, and pay for everything in cash. When the envelope is empty, you're done shopping. You can also use a series of envelopes, one for each budget category.

Now that we have our terms straight, let's give a go at filling in some of those blanks.

Element	Cost
Total Budget	$350.00
Invitations	$
Venue	$
Food	$
Drink	$
Tools	$
Décor	$
Entertainment/Activities	$
Music	$
Favors	$
Emergency Fund	$35.00
Total Costs	$

I can safely spend $350 on this party, $35 of which I'll set aside for emergencies. Before we can fill in any more blanks, we'll need to consider a few variables.

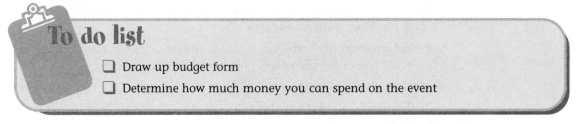

To do list

☐ Draw up budget form

☐ Determine how much money you can spend on the event

Setting a Party Date

Looking at my calendar, May seems like a good time for my next party. It's not quite summer, but late enough in the year that it will be warm in the evening. I prefer a Saturday afternoon/evening party, which will give me most of the day to prepare and a whole day to recover. At the end of the month, I'll be visiting my grandmother in another state, so the first two weeks will be best for the party.

Let's say the first Saturday in May, at about four o'clock. We'll have plenty of daylight until about seven o'clock, after which the party will continue until everyone goes home. I don't need an ending time because I will have all day Sunday to sleep, clean, and laze about.

Final party date: Saturday, May 4 at 4:00 p.m.

Before you set your date, take a good look at your work and personal calendars. Do you have any big deadlines coming up at work? Are other friends hosting parties or events? Avoid over committing yourself, and you'll save yourself a lot of stress.

Choosing a Theme

As it happens, Cinco de Mayo, Mexican Independence Day, is May 5, which coincides nicely with my party theme. I happen to love cooking Mexican food, and Mexican-themed parties are always fun—plus, they're cheap!

> **tip** Tying in your party to a holiday is a great way to add a fun theme when you're operating on a lower budget. If you were a smart shopper, you picked up a bunch of stuff at last year's after-holiday sales, so you'll already have a head-start on décor. If not, you'll be able to find plenty at inexpensive party stores, discount shops, and dollar stores.

Deciding on the Party's Venue

Because I have a large backyard with a fairly nice patio and grill, I'll have the party at my house. I won't need to rent any chairs or tables, and I can clean my house myself, so I don't have to enter anything into the budget sheet except a big, fat zero.

Although many rented venues will supply everything you need to host a party, not everything will be to your liking or standards. If you're shelling out big bucks to host a party in a lovely space, make sure you are getting your money's worth! Ask to see linens, dishes, décor, and anything else you'd like to be in top shape.

Drawing Up the Guest List

I usually invite about 50 people to my parties, of which 40 or so actually show up. I'll plan for 50, though, just in case I get stragglers, surprise-shows, or posses.

Because my party will be a big mixer, with folks eating and drinking and socializing, I'm not afraid to invite people from disparate groups. My guest list will include people from my book group, my writing group, the dog park, a few

> **tip** 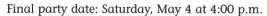 If you're going to try to fix up any of your friends, do yourself a favor and let them know ahead of time. If both parties are aware they'll be meeting a potential date, they can plan ahead and arrive with a cute outfit and an open mind. You won't have to spend as much time at the party talking your friends into talking to one another.

neighbors, several of my husband's work friends, about a dozen couples we know, and all my single girlfriends, of course! I'll let people know they can bring friends, as long as they give me an idea of how many people they're bringing.

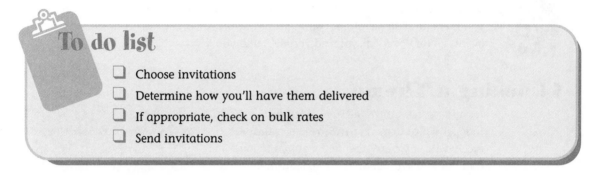

To do list

- ☐ Choose invitations
- ☐ Determine how you'll have them delivered
- ☐ If appropriate, check on bulk rates
- ☐ Send invitations

Sending Out Invitations

Although sending out handwritten invitations would be a cute touch, especially if I could find Cinco de Mayo invites, I think it would be wasted money for this particular party. With 50 invited guests, the postage alone would eat a hole in my budget!

Instead, I'll use a web-based invitation system to notify my guests. I prefer Evite (www.evite.com) because I have been using it for years with great success. Without trying to sound like a spokesperson for the company, I can say that using Evite enables me to invite everyone in my address book, customize my invitations with a Mexican theme, include all the details (date, time, and location), and track my guests' responses. I can keep an eye on how many people are planning to come and adjust my shopping list accordingly.

tip If you prefer to send out invitations, check with your post office to see if you are inviting enough people to qualify for a bulk rate. Although you don't want to go this route for weddings or other occasions for which presentation counts, there's nothing wrong with using bulk mail for your Halloween party invites!

Best of all, Evite is free! I won't have to spend a dime on invitations or postage, so I'll enter another zero on the budget sheet.

You'll Need

- ❑ Guest list and contact information
- ❑ Computer and Internet access (if sending electronically)
- ❑ Printed invitations and postage (if sending through mail)

Planning the Party Food

I love making Mexican food! It's easy, the ingredients are relatively inexpensive, and Mexican cuisine is well suited to a buffet, which is perfect for a larger party. Mexican food is also great for a mix of people, some of whom might be vegetarian.

I have a great recipe for carnitas and fish tostadas, which use similar condiments and vegetables. I can save time by making only two meat dishes and using the same sides for both.

My menu will include

- Carnitas (2 × the recipe = 16 servings)
- Tilapia Tostados (2 × normal recipe = 24 servings)
- Grilled Vegetables (zucchini, red bell peppers)
- Iptacita's Guacamole (2 × normal recipe = 24 servings)
- Dee's Bean Dip (2 × normal recipe = 24 servings)
- Chips and Fresh Salsa
- Cream Cheese Brownies (3 × normal recipe = 48 brownies)

This might not sound like a lot of food, but the two dips and two entrees are satisfying and can be combined in a lot of different ways, which should allow my guests to be creative with their food selections. The grilled zucchini and red bell peppers will add more nutrition to the menu and will give vegetarians some "meat" for their tostados.

When you're planning any party menu, remember to take into account your guests' different diets. Because so many people are going low-carb or vegetarian these days, you might run into problems finding a menu that everyone can enjoy. The menu I've selected for the sample party includes a lot of vegetables, as well as a main course that can be eaten with or without carb-laden bread or tortillas.

You'll Need

- ❑ Party menu
- ❑ Recipes
- ❑ List-making materials

Making a Shopping List

Now that I know what I'm going to make, I need to take a look at the ingredients lists and make a shopping list, which will help me figure out how much money I need to budget for food. I'm hoping to only need about $100.

I'll start by taking a look at the ingredients for each dish and seeing what ingredients overlap. (You can find these recipes on our website at www.quepublishing.com.)

As I go through each recipe, I'll make a list of each ingredient, and then adjust the quantities accordingly as they overlap. Here's what my ingredients list will look like (note that I'm keeping track of what I already have on hand):

Ingredients	Quantity	On Hand?
Pork shoulder	10 lbs.	
Onions	4	
Celery stalks	4	
Carrots	4	
Frozen orange juice concentrate	1 can	
Garlic bulbs	2	
Bay leaves	4	X
Chili chipotle	1 7-oz. can	
Ground cumin	2 tsp.	X
Coriander	2 tsp.	X
Mexican spice thyme	2 tsp.	X
Salt	4 T	X
Whole peppercorns	2 T	X
Chicken broth	2 large cans	
Milk	2 C	
Corn tortillas	4 packages	
Salsa	2 pts.	
Sour cream	1 pt.	

Ingredients	Quantity	On Hand?
Shredded Mexican blend cheese	28 C	
Avocados	10	
Fresh cilantro	3 C	
Tilapia	6 lbs.	
Plain yogurt	4 C	
Sugar	4 C	X
Chili powder	½ tsp.	X
Limes	12	
Shredded cabbage	1 large package	
Fat-free refried beans	4 cans	
Taco seasoning	2 pkgs.	
Cream cheese	16 oz.	
Chopped green chilies	2 small cans	
Chopped black olives	2 small cans	
Serrano peppers	6	
Olive oil	1 C	
Zucchini	1 lb.	
Red bell peppers	4	
Butter	1 pkg.	
Marshmallow cream	3 jars	
Evaporated milk	3 small cans	
Vanilla	3 tsp.	X
Semi-sweet chocolate chips	18 oz.	

After seeing what I have already in my kitchen, I can make a final shopping list, estimating what everything will cost and sorting the list according to grocery-store placement, for easier shopping:

Ingredients	Quantity	Cost
Pork shoulder	10 lbs.	$40.00
Tilapia	6 lbs.	10.00
Onions	4	2.00
Celery stalks	4	1.00
Carrots	4	1.00
Shredded cabbage	1 large pkg.	4.00

continues

Ingredients	Quantity	Cost
Zucchini	1 lb.	3.00
Red bell peppers	4	4.00
Serrano peppers	6	2.00
Avocados	10	10.00
Limes	12	1.20
Fresh cilantro	3 C	2.10
Garlic bulbs	2	.75
Salsa	2 pts.	8.00
Sour cream	1 pt.	2.00
Cream cheese	16 oz.	2.10
Plain yogurt	4 C	4.00
Milk	2 C	2.00
Butter	1 pkg.	4.50
Shredded Mexican cheese	28 C	10.00
Frozen orange juice concentrate	1 can	2.50
Corn tortillas	4 pkgs.	6.00
Chili chipotle	1 7-oz. can	1.50
Chopped green chilies	2 small cans	1.00
Chopped black olives	2 small cans	1.00
Chicken broth	2 large cans	2.50
Fat-free refried beans	4 cans	1.50
Taco seasoning	2 pkgs.	2.00
Marshmallow cream	3 jars	6.00
Evaporated milk	3 small cans	1.50
Semi-sweet chocolate chips	15 oz.	2.50
Tortilla chips	3 bags	6.00
Total		**$147.65**

Calculating Final Costs

I plan to do my shopping at Costco, which is my local warehouse store, where I hope to get many of the ingredients at a lower price.

Save your local supermarket circulars for a few weeks before your party so you can compare prices. Although most cities have a variety of low-cost warehouse store options (Wal-Mart, Costco, and Sam's Club), you will not be able to find everything at these stores and will need to shop at a regular store for at least a few of the ingredients. The more money you save on food, the more you have left for other party fun, such as liquor!

I can now fill in the Food element on my budget chart:

Element	Cost
Total Budget	$350.00
Venue	0.00
Invitations	0.00
Food	150.00
Drink	
Tools	
Décor	
Entertainment/Activities	
Music	
Favors	
Emergency Fund	35.00
Total Costs	

Yikes! That doesn't leave a lot of money left for the rest of the party. I'd better take a careful look at what beverages I want to serve.

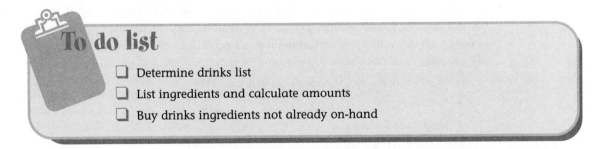

To do list

- ❏ Determine drinks list
- ❏ List ingredients and calculate amounts
- ❏ Buy drinks ingredients not already on-hand

Stocking Up on Beverages

The Mexican theme requires margaritas and Mexican beer, but I don't think I can afford both, as well as soft drinks, water, and ice. I'd like to get a keg, but I definitely can't afford *that*. I need to find a way to offer great booze, but keep the beverage budget as low as possible.

I'd love to have a tequila tasting, in which guests would each bring a different bottle of tequila to share, but I don't want to ask my friends to shell out a ton of money. Instead, I'll have a Mexican beer tasting. I'll invite guests to bring a six-pack of their favorite Mexican beer, and recruit three or four tasters to sample each beer. We can make a production of it, with blindfolds, a tasting table, and an emcee...this idea could really work!

Not only will this beer tasting cut down beverage costs tremendously, but it will clue guests in on what to bring for a hostess gift, and we can include the tasting as part of the entertainment. Sure, some people won't bring the beer, and others will bring duplicates, but it will all work out.

I can use a medium-priced tequila for the margaritas, which will save money. You don't need to purchase top-shelf tequila when you're making margaritas, unless you are hosting a very small party. Really, who's going to know? If you feel embarrassed, just decant the tequila into a vintage glass bottle. You can pretend you are being a classy host.

According to my calculations, I will be hosting about 50 people, at least 40 of whom will drink. Hearkening back to what we learned in Chapter 3, "Party Basics," plan for two drinks per person for the first two hours of the party, and then one drink per person for every hour thereafter. Because the party will last about 5 hours, I will need to plan about 280 drinks. Again, yikes!

A 1.5-liter bottle of tequila is equivalent to about 50 ounces, and each margarita requires 1.5 ounces of tequila. Therefore, each bottle will yield about 34 margaritas. Because we'll be featuring beer, soda, and water, and because tequila drinkers tend to only have a few drinks before switching to beer, I think that three 1.5-liter bottles will be enough. That's about 100 margaritas, if you are keeping track.

Here's what my Beverages shopping list will look like:

• Tequila (4.5 L)	$40.00
• Triple sec (.75 L)	7.00
• Sour mix (1 bottle)	5.00
• Fresh limes (36)	5.00
• Margarita salt	3.00
• Corona (1 case)	20.00
• Pepsi (12-pack)	5.00

- Diet Pepsi (12-pack)   5.00
- Bottled water (case)   5.00
- Ice (5 bags)   5.00

It's going to be tight, but I think I can pull it off. If I can get a deal, or if I have anything left over from my food budget, I'll pick up a bottle of top-shelf tequila, which I can pull out if we want to do a couple shots.

Okay! Enough math. My drinks budget will look like this:

Element	Cost
Total Budget	$350.00
Venue	0.00
Invitations	0.00
Food	150.00
Drink	100.00
Tools	
Décor	
Entertainment/Activities	
Music	
Favors	
Emergency Fund	35.00
Total Costs	

That leaves about $65 left for the rest of the party, which I don't think will be a problem. My party is going to be on the kitschy side, so I won't need to invest a lot in décor or favors. In fact, the cheaper the better!

To do list

- ❏ Create list of supplies, equipment, and other tools you'll need to prepare/serve food and accommodate party guests
- ❏ Check on-hand stock of necessary tools (both availability and condition)
- ❏ Acquire tools not on-hand

Gathering the Necessary Tools

After planning out the food and drinks, I have a good idea of what I'll need to make this party work. My budget for tools will be minimal; I already have a grill, and there's plenty of propane in the tank. I have all the tools I'll need to prepare and serve all the food and drinks—I even have a blender in case someone insists on a blended margarita!

I already have all the candles anyone could ever want, including tea lights, votive candles, and tapers, all in white—which is one of the colors of the Mexican flag. I have about a dozen tiki torches and enough oil to last the night; plus, we have red chili-pepper lights strung in the backyard, so lighting is all set.

I have red-and-white checkered tablecloths for the kitchen, patio, and picnic tables, and I picked up a ton of white dinner napkins at a sale last year. I'll need to buy clear, plastic cups and utensils, as well as small and large paper plates. I can get all of that at Costco or a discount store for about $20.

I will need two large, plastic buckets—one for the beer and the other for the soda and water. I'll fill the buckets with ice and let guests help themselves. I happen to know that I can pick up plastic buckets (red, even, which will go nicely with my theme) for $4.99 each, so my shopping list will look like this:

- Red plastic buckets (2) $10.00
- Cups   5.00
- Utensils   5.00
- Small plates   5.00
- Large plates   5.00

A week or two before you throw a party, it's a good idea to take inventory of your kitchen and make sure you have everything you'll need to prepare and serve the food and drinks, including tools, gadgets, electronics, serving dishes, and cookware. The last thing you want is to be in the middle of preparing your carnitas, only to find you don't have the right pot in which to cook them! So, I'd better start keeping track of the stuff I'll need to get out of storage or borrow, just to make sure I don't forget anything, here's a list:

I'll Need

- Candles
- Checkered tablecloths
- Tiki torches and oil

tip If your kitchen does fall short of complete, don't blow a huge chunk of your budget before the party. Check out your local dollar store and see if you can get inexpensive items that you can later substitute for quality tools.

Before the party, I'll make sure that I actually have all this stuff and that it is clean and in working order.

I can also update my budget sheet:

Element	Cost
Total Budget	$350.00
Venue	0.00
Invitations	0.00
Food	150.00
Drink	100.00
Tools	30.00
Décor	
Entertainment/Activities	
Music	
Favors	
Emergency Fund	35.00
Total Costs	

To do list

- ☐ Think about repurposing items you already have into party décor
- ☐ Calculate what additional decorations you can purchase within your budget
- ☐ Create list of all decorations you'll use
- ☐ Add appropriate items to shopping list and budget sheet
- ☐ Acquire decorations

Decorating for the Party

Here's when the real fun begins: decorating! Because almost no one does it anymore, I happen to love decorating for parties. I tend to lean toward the kitsch, selecting super-cheap décor that makes people laugh.

I only have $35 left in my budget, so I'll have to be creative. My friend, Ben, has a full-sized Mexican flag, so I'll hang that from the edge of the porch in the backyard, which is where most of the party will take place. Another friend of mine collects sombreros (I don't know why), so I will beg him to loan them to me for the party. I have about five Mexican blankets, which I can spread on the grass in case anyone wants to sit. I picked up a bunch of Mexican saints candles a few months ago (I liked the kitschy labels), so I can use those to anchor down the tablecloths and decorate the food table.

I'd better add to my list of stuff to get ready:

I'll Need

- Candles
- Checkered tablecloths
- Tiki torches and oil
- Mexican flag (Ben)
- Sombreros (Tony)
- Mexican blankets
- Saints candles

Because the budget is so small, and because I want to save about $25 for the favors, that means I only have $10 for the décor. Bummer! It's a good thing most of my décor is either free or in my party closet.

I can pick up some helium balloons in red, white, and green (the colors of the Mexican flag) and tie them in clumps around the back fence. I think the balloons will only cost about $5, so I guess I'll use the remaining $5 to buy a piñata. I really hope I can find one for that price, or else I'll have to dip into the emergency fund, which is a big no-no.

 As you're planning your décor, don't be afraid to get creative, as I've done for this party. Scour discount stores and closeout sales for themed items that you normally wouldn't buy, even for $.99. A cracked, heart-shaped bowl can make a great centerpiece for a Valentine's Day party: Just use it for flowers, and you won't notice the flaws.

Okay, I think that's it for the décor. Here's my shopping list:

- Balloons $5.00
- Piñata   5.00

And to update my budget sheet:

Element	Cost
Total Budget	$350.00
Venue	0.00
Invitations	0.00
Food	150.00
Drink	100.00
Tools	30.00
Décor	10.00
Entertainment/Activities	
Music	
Favors	
Emergency Fund	35.00
Total Costs	

Well, I don't have as much décor as I'd like, but the most important elements for this particular party are the food and beverages, which will be great. The backyard is in good shape, with a lot of flowers already blooming, so I'll have to let nature be my decorator and let the Mexican details lend atmosphere.

note If you're planning an outdoor party, think *way* ahead. Plants and flowers do require time to bloom and flourish, so if you're planning a June garden party, start planting in early spring.

Planning Entertainment or Activities

I already have two activities planned—the beer tasting and the piñata. I don't think this party will go well if I try to impose a lot of structure, so I'll plan to have the beer tasting about two hours into the party, at 6:00 p.m., with dinner to follow. At about 8:00 p.m., we'll do the piñata. By that time, everyone will be loose and relaxed—hopefully not so "relaxed" that they'll beat each other while trying to break the piñata!

Although I've planned the activities for particular times, I won't stress about them on the day of the party. As guests arrive and get comfortable, I'll keep an eye on the energy level and bust out the activities when I think the party needs a boost.

My budget for Entertainment/Activities: $0!

I really wish I could have hired a Mariachi band, but I just can't afford it. Hmm…I wonder if any of my guitar-playing friends know any Mexican songs?

Don't be a Monica. Although the *Friends* character was organized and impeccable, she could also be a royal pain when she hosted a party. Remember the scene in which she yelled at her guests for not capping the pens tightly enough during her stuffy party game? Let your guests' energy and enthusiasm dictate when and how your planned activities happen. If no one wants to play the fabulous word game you prepared, let it slide. The activities are meant to entertain guests, not enslave them.

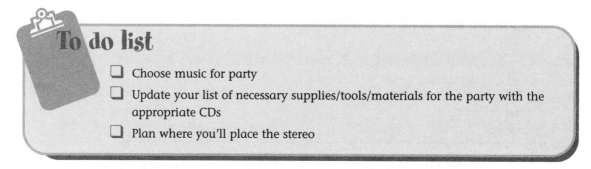

To do list

❑ Choose music for party

❑ Update your list of necessary supplies/tools/materials for the party with the appropriate CDs

❑ Plan where you'll place the stereo

Choosing the Right Music

A Mexican party calls for Mexican music. I don't want to drive my guests crazy by playing nonstop Mariachi, so I'll set a stack of CDs next to the stereo and let people change the music if they wish. However, I'll get together a few theme-appropriate CDs, which I'll have playing as the guests arrive. Later on, we can switch to classic rock, which will go nicely with the atmosphere: beer, margaritas, and relaxing.

From my collection, I can pull out these CDs for the party:

- The *Frida* Soundtrack
- *Mariachi from Mexico*
- *Selena's Greatest Hits*
- *Rough Guide to the Music of Mexico*
- Kronos Quartet, *Neuvo*

I don't own any salsa music, which will be good for later in the night, but a couple of my friends do. I'll ask them to bring over the CDs a few days before the party, just so I make sure I have them on the big day.

Although I won't need to update my budget sheet, I will need to add to my "I'll Need" list:

I'll Need

- Candles
- Checkered tablecloths
- Tiki torches and oil
- Mexican flag (Ben)
- Sombreros (Tony)
- Mexican blankets
- Saints candles
- Mexican CDs
- Classic rock CDs
- Salsa CDs (Andrea and Kylee)

My stereo is in good shape; I'll move it just outside the back doors, which lead from the living room to the backyard. That way, my guests can hear the music in the house and in the yard. I'll keep the remote in my pocket, just in case someone puts something really heinous on the CD player. I'm all set!

Don't force your guests to listen to lame music! If you can't afford to purchase music for your party and you don't have what you need in your CD library, ask your friends to loan you a few discs, check out music resale stores, or visit the library. Your music will create constant atmosphere throughout your party, so make sure you have music your guests will love.

To do list

- ❑ Choose party favors that will fit within your budget
- ❑ Acquire the favors
- ❑ Determine where and how to place them

Buying Great (but Cheap!) Party Favors

One last budget item remains: party favors. This is my absolute favorite thing to buy, mostly because no one ever gives out favors unless they are getting married. Favors are fun and silly, especially at a party like this one. Although I wish I had more money to spend on them, I can pick up some great stuff for $25.

I live in Southern California, home to a huge Hispanic population. About a week before the party, I'll hit a couple of stores downtown and pick up a bunch of toys: string dolls, Mexican yo-yos, firecrackers, maracas, silly string, and whatever else I can find that costs between $.25 and $1 each. I'll put everything in a big bowl near the booze, and people can take what they like.

Although favors are fun, they are not absolutely essential to your party. If you really can't afford to spend the extra money, don't. Ultimately, the food and drink are the most important, with ambience coming in a close second. Spend your money where it counts, and then opt for frills, such as favors, only if your budget allows.

Checking Over Your Final Budget, Shopping, and Tools Lists

At last, my budget sheet is complete! Here's what the final budget looks like:

Element	Cost
Total Budget	$350.00
Venue	0.00
Invitations	0.00
Food	150.00
Drink	100.00
Tools	30.00
Décor	10.00
Entertainment/Activities	0.00
Music	0.00
Favors	25.00
Emergency Fund	35.00
Total Costs	**$350.00**

I still have $35 left over in the emergency fund, so if any disasters happen, I'm covered. If I still have the extra money the day of the party, after I've bought everything on my list, I'll spring for that bottle of top-shelf tequila!

Do try to include at least one quality element in your party planning—a fine dessert, a premium liquor, or a rich appetizer. Even if the rest of your elements are bargain-basement, your guests will remember the extra touch and associate your party with quality.

To review, we made two other lists besides the budget. Here's our final "I'll Need" list:

I'll Need

- Candles
- Checkered tablecloths
- Tiki torches and oil
- Mexican flag (Ben)
- Sombreros (Tony)
- Mexican blankets
- Saints candles
- Mexican CDs
- Classic rock CDs
- Salsa CDs (Andrea and Kylee)

And our final shopping list:

Ingredients	Quantity	Cost
Pork shoulder	10 lbs.	$40.00
Tilapia	6 lbs.	10.00
Onions	4	2.00
Celery stalks	4	1.00
Carrots	4	1.00
Shredded cabbage	1 large pkg.	4.00
Zucchini	1 lb.	3.00
Red bell peppers	4	4.00
Serrano peppers	6	2.00
Avocados	10	10.00
Limes	48	5.00
Fresh cilantro	3 C	2.10
Garlic bulbs	2	.75
Salsa	2 pts.	8.00
Sour cream	1 pt.	2.00
Cream cheese	16 oz.	2.10

continues

Ingredients	Quantity	Cost
Plain yogurt	4 C	4.00
Milk	2 C	2.00
Butter	1 pkg.	4.50
Shredded Mexican cheese	28 C	10.00
Frozen orange juice concentrate	1 can	2.50
Corn tortillas	4 pkgs.	6.00
Chili chipotle	1 7-oz. can	1.50
Chopped green chilies	2 small cans	1.00
Chopped black olives	2 small cans	1.00
Chicken broth	2 large cans	2.50
Fat-free refried beans	4 cans	1.50
Taco seasoning	2 pkgs.	2.00
Marshmallow cream	3 jars	6.00
Evaporated milk	3 small cans	1.50
Semi-sweet chocolate chips	15 oz.	2.50
Tortilla chips	3 bags	6.00
Tequila (1.5 L)	3 bottles	40.00
Triple sec (.75 L)	1 bottle	7.00
Sour mix	1 bottle	5.00
Margarita salt	1 tub	3.00
Corona	1 case	20.00
Pepsi	12-pack	5.00
Diet Pepsi	12-pack	5.00
Bottled water	1 case	5.00
Ice	5 bags	5.00

Although it took a while to make these three lists, we've just planned the *entire* party. Considering everything that was involved, it took no time at all!

Summary

In this chapter, we planned out a complete party. We decided on a budget, selected a date and time, picked a theme, confirmed the venue, decided on the guest list, thought out the invitations, planned the food and drink menu, made sure we had all the tools we needed, decided on décor, planned activities and music, and selected favors. We also made three lists, which we'll use in the next chapter: our shopping list, our budget sheet, and our "I'll Need" list. In the next chapter, you'll learn how to translate the three lists into tasks we'll accomplish during the weeks before the party. By doing a little bit of work here and there, we'll only have the setup and cooking to do the day of the party.

Counting Down

6

Now that you've learned how to plan out your party, the next step is making it happen. To keep yourself stress-free on the big day, you'll need to learn how to turn your careful planning into simple tasks you can perform days ahead of the party date. We'll look at why it's important to plan ahead, how to create task lists, how to combine them into a master checklist, and how to schedule tasks so you get everything wrapped up long before your first guest arrives.

You'll Need

❑ The shopping and "I'll Need" lists you made in Chapter 5, "Planning Ahead"

❑ A pencil and your party notebook (or your computer!)

❑ A positive attitude!

Doing It Ahead!

As you are racing around, trying to get everything done before your guests arrive, try to remember your goal for this event: to ensure you and your guests have a great time. If you become a scary person, you will suck all the fun out of your own party, leaving your guests to wonder why you bothered to have them over.

In this chapter:

✳ Understand the value of planning ahead so you aren't frazzled the day of your party

✳ Learn how to turn your to-do and shopping lists into easily managed task lists

✳ Figure out how to schedule each task, so you aren't overwhelmed in the days leading up to your party

✳ Find out how to create a master checklist that will guide you through the day of your party

Although I might sound like your mother, I'll take the risk: Don't leave everything to the last minute! With a little planning ahead, you can ease into your party day, feeling a sense of excitement you'll be able to pass onto your guests.

Schedule your planning so that bathing isn't the very last thing you plan to do before the party begins. Chances are good that you'll find too many last-minute things to do, won't have time to bathe, and wind up greeting your guests with a less-than-attractive appearance (and odor!). Instead, schedule a good personal cleanup about two hours before the guests are due to arrive. Light a few candles and take a long, hot shower or bath, using good-smelling products that invigorate your senses. Dress and groom yourself, and then take care of your last-minute preparations. You'll greet your guests feeling relaxed and happy, instead of stressed-out and smelly.

Remember, a calm, confident approach is the core of successful hosting. If you achieve inner peace before your party, you'll be able to pull off the entire event with aplomb, handling little emergencies with unflappable grace. You'll have a better time, and your guests will have more fun if they aren't helping you manage your stress level.

To-Do Lists

In Chapter 5, we created three party-planning aids:

- A budget
- An "I'll Need" list of party tools, supplies, and so on
- A shopping list

In creating these lists, you already alleviated a lot of the stress that goes into throwing a party. You know what you need and how much everything should cost. The next step is taking care of everything on those lists, in a calm, organized, and efficient manner.

To do list

- ❑ Put your shopping list to use as we track down the ingredients we'll need for our party
- ❑ Brainstorm a list of tasks that need to be completed before the party

The Shopping List

The easiest way to figure out *how* I'm going to get everything to my house in enough time to prepare for the party is to figure out *where* I'm going to purchase everything. I'll add a column to my shopping list, identifying which store I'm going to need to visit for each ingredient, and then sort the list by the stores I'll visit. I'll also add a column for checking off each item as I track it down.

> **tip**
> You'll save yourself a lot of time and effort if you use a computer for your shopping and task lists. You can use either word-processing or spreadsheet software, which will enable you to manipulate your lists without having to retype or rewrite everything a million times.

For the lowest prices on bulk items, I'll go to Costco, my local warehouse store (also try Smart & Final, Sam's Club, or Wal-Mart). I know Costco has the best prices on fresh meat, bulk vegetables and cheese, soda, water, and liquor. Even though the trip might take a little longer than I'd like, as I fight my way through a sea of shoppers, my savings on these items, especially the meat, will make the trip worthwhile.

For grocery items, I'll visit Trader Joe's, which has a great selection of fresh, interesting foods at low prices. Because I've been shopping at this store for years, I'm very familiar with its stock and prices, and I know exactly what I can buy there at a lower cost than a traditional supermarket. I'll visit a discount supermarket for the few items I can't find at Trader Joe's.

For the ice buckets, I'll visit Smart & Final, a warehouse-style store that sells bulk items at really low prices. I can also get my paper plates, cups, and eating utensils at Smart & Final. If you don't have a Smart & Final near you, check dollar stores for these items. If you can't find them there, a regular party store or supermarket will have to do.

> **note**
> With stores across the United States, Trader Joe's is an inexpensive grocery-type store that sells almost everything you'll find at a regular grocery store, at much lower prices. If you don't have a Trader Joe's near you, you can shop at a discount grocery store for bulk items, or adjust your budget to allow for regular grocery-store prices.

With quick trips to the Mexican market for the favors and piñata, and the party store for the balloons, my party shopping will be finished.

Even though it's prudent to accomplish as much as you can as far ahead of time as possible, don't shortchange your guests! You'll want your food items to be fresh, which means you can't get them until, at most, three or four days ahead of time—and only two days for produce and fish. Likewise, if you're decorating with balloons or flowers, you should get them the day before the party or they might not be as perky as you'd like. As you think about your task list, keep quality and freshness in mind, and plan accordingly.

Here's our revised shopping list. I can simply print off this list and take it with me to the stores I'll need to visit. The ingredients are still in order of store sections (dairy, produce, and so forth), so getting in and out with everything on my list will be a snap.

I can also stay on budget by ignoring everything in the store that isn't on my list, and just checking off each item as I put it in the cart. Although I might be tempted to toss in an extra treat or two, my shopping list helps me stay focused.

✔	Ingredients	Quantity	Cost	Store
	Pork shoulder	10 lbs.	$40.00	Costco
	Shredded cabbage	1 large pkg.	4.00	Costco
	Zucchini	1 lb.	3.00	Costco
	Shredded Mexican cheese	28 C	10.00	Costco
	Corn tortillas	4 pkgs.	6.00	Costco
	Tortilla chips	3 bags	6.00	Costco
	Tequila (1.5 L)	3 bottles	40.00	Costco
	Corona	1 case	20.00	Costco
	Pepsi	12-pack	5.00	Costco
	Diet Pepsi	12-pack	5.00	Costco
	Bottled water	1 case	5.00	Costco
	Cups	4 dozen	5.00	Costco
	Utensils	4 dozen sets	5.00	Costco
	Small plates	4 dozen	5.00	Costco
	Large plates	4 dozen	5.00	Costco
	Serrano peppers	6	2.00	Grocery store
	Chopped green chilies	2 small cans	1.00	Grocery store
	Chopped black olives	2 small cans	1.00	Grocery store
	Fat-free refried beans	4 cans	1.50	Grocery store
	Taco seasoning	2 pkgs.	2.00	Grocery store
	Marshmallow cream	3 jars	6.00	Grocery store
	Evaporated milk	3 small cans	1.50	Grocery store
	Margarita salt	1 tub	3.00	Grocery store
	Ice	5 bags	5.00	Grocery store

✔	Ingredients	Quantity	Cost	Store
	Red plastic buckets	2	10.00	Smart & Final
	Cups		5.00	Smart & Final
	Utensils		5.00	Smart & Final
	Small plates		5.00	Smart & Final
	Large plates		5.00	Smart & Final
	Piñata	1	5.00	Mexican market
	Favors		25.00	Mexican market
	Balloons	About 15	5.00	Party store
	Tilapia	6 lbs.	10.00	Trader Joe's
	Onions	4	2.00	Trader Joe's
	Celery stalks	4	1.00	Trader Joe's
	Carrots	4	1.00	Trader Joe's
	Red bell peppers	4	4.00	Trader Joe's
	Avocados	10	10.00	Trader Joe's
	Limes	48	5.00	Trader Joe's
	Fresh cilantro	3 C	2.10	Trader Joe's
	Garlic bulbs	2	.75	Trader Joe's
	Salsa	2 pts.	8.00	Trader Joe's
	Sour cream	1 pt.	2.00	Trader Joe's
	Cream cheese	16 oz.	2.10	Trader Joe's
	Plain yogurt	4 C	4.00	Trader Joe's
	Milk	2 C	2.00	Trader Joe's
	Butter	1 pkg.	4.50	Trader Joe's
	Frozen orange juice concentrate	1 can	2.50	Trader Joe's
	Chili chipotle	1 7-oz. can	1.50	Trader Joe's
	Chicken broth	2 large cans	2.50	Trader Joe's
	Semi-sweet chocolate chips	15 oz.	2.50	Trader Joe's
	Triple sec (.75 L)	1 bottle	7.00	Trader Joe's
	Sour mix	1 bottle	5.00	Trader Joe's

This list might seem overly detailed, but it will save you a *lot* of time. By identifying everything you need, as well as where you'll need to go to get it, you can take a long, scary-looking shopping list and identify just a few manageable store trips. With that in mind, you can plan out the weeks before the party, scheduling these trips at times that are convenient to your schedule, thereby reducing your stress level before you even begin. The next step is to identify the tasks you'll need to take care of if you want the party to be a smash.

The To-Do List

When you're thinking about the work you'll need to do before the big day, chances are good that your brain will start spinning and your stomach will start clenching. That's what happens to me when I mentally survey everything a party requires.

As soon as my body protests ("Another party? *Why?*"), I just take a deep breath and remind myself how much fun I always have, not just the day of the party, but getting everything ready. Then I sit down at my computer and brainstorm everything I'll need to do. I find that getting tasks out of my head and onto the computer screen helps calm my nerves as I realize that it *is* possible to get everything done in time.

Here's my brainstorming list, in the order that each task occurs to me. Make your own list as I make mine, as your home and mine will differ.

To do list

- ☐ Visit Trader Joe's
- ☐ Visit party store
- ☐ Visit Costco
- ☐ Visit Mexican market
- ☐ Visit Smart & Final
- ☐ Visit grocery store
- ☐ Clean bathroom
- ☐ Clean kitchen
- ☐ Sweep floors
- ☐ Dust and tidy house
- ☐ Empty trash and recycling
- ☐ Pick up dog deposits
- ☐ Change cat litter box
- ☐ Launder clothing
- ☐ Launder rugs
- ☐ Tidy yards
- ☐ Check propane and clean grill
- ☐ Clean patio furniture
- ☐ Send out invitations
- ☐ Get items on "I'll Need" list
- ☐ Move stereo
- ☐ Select party CDs
- ☐ Decorate party areas
- ☐ Get myself ready for the party
- ☐ Feed and walk dogs
- ☐ Prepare food
- ☐ Prepare beverages
- ☐ Set up party tools
- ☐ Clean out fridge

Wow, that's a lot of stuff to do! However, from past experience, I know I can do it all. First, I'll need to figure out when!

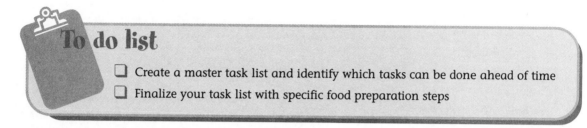

To do list

❏ Create a master task list and identify which tasks can be done ahead of time
❏ Finalize your task list with specific food preparation steps

Mastering Your Task List

The easiest way to take care of everything on this to-do list is to figure out the best time to do everything, and schedule my calendar so that I'm not overwhelmed by tasks, but rather take care of a few each day.

Planning It Out

Here's where using a computer comes in really handy. I'll turn my to-do list into a little chart, noting which tasks need to be accomplished the month before the party, the week before, two days before, the day before, and the actual day of the party.

Here's my chart:

Task	Month Before	Week Before	Two Days Before	Day Before	Party Day
Visit Trader Joe's			X		
Visit party store				X	
Visit Costco			X		
Visit Mexican market	X				
Visit grocery store				X	
Visit Smart & Final	X				
Clean bathroom				X	
Clean kitchen				X	
Sweep floors					X
Dust and tidy house					X
Empty trash and recycling					X

continues

Task	Month Before	Week Before	Two Days Before	Day Before	Party Day
Pick up dog deposits					X
Change cat litter box				X	
Launder clothing				X	
Launder rugs				X	
Tidy yards				X	
Check propane and clean grill		X			
Clean patio furniture					X
Send out invitations	X				
Get items on "I'll Need" list		X			
Move stereo					X
Select party CDs		X			
Decorate party areas					X
Get myself ready for the party					X
Feed and walk dogs					X
Prepare food				X	X
Prepare beverages					X
Set up party tools					X
Clean out fridge		X			

Okay, that's much more manageable!

Everything in Good Time

My next step is to sort the table by when I need to take care of each task. Before I do that, however, I'll need to take a look at the recipes I'm preparing and determine what can be done ahead.

We've decided to make the following recipes (which you can find on our web site www.quepublishing.com:

- Carnitas
- Tilapia Tostados
- Grilled Vegetables (zucchini, red bell peppers)

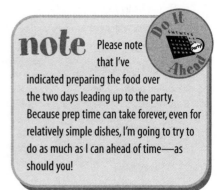

note Please note that I've indicated preparing the food over the two days leading up to the party. Because prep time can take forever, even for relatively simple dishes, I'm going to try to do as much as I can ahead of time—as should you!

- Iptacita's Guacamole
- Dee's Bean Dip
- Chips and Salsa
- Cream Cheese Brownies

We're planning to make a number of recipes, so I'll have to take a careful look at the different preparation steps and determine how long each step will take.

I'll start with the meat: The carnitas recipe needs to slow-cook overnight and requires a couple of different steps the day of the party. The fish for the tilapia tostados needs to be prepared just before serving. I'd like the food to be ready by about 5:30 p.m., which will give all my guests a chance to arrive, get comfortable, and socialize a little before dinner, so I'll need to plan my cooking time accordingly.

Looking at the two recipes, many of the garnishes overlap. I think I'll save myself some time by altering the tostada recipe to skip the tortilla-frying step. My guests can assemble pork or fish in the same corn tortillas, turning the tostadas into soft tacos. I'll save a lot of time that way!

I'll prepare all the garnishes the night before, chopping everything and leaving it refrigerated in sealed plastic containers until dinnertime.

Looking at the next items on the menu, I can also chop the grilled vegetables the night before and make the brownies. Although they would be delicious served hot, they'll be almost as good the next day, and cooking them the night before will help me out with my schedule. The guacamole might get icky if I fix it the day before, so I'll wait until the party day. It doesn't take very long to mix up; neither does the bean dip, which I'll make that day, as well. The chips and salsa won't take more than a minute to pour into festive serving bowls.

caution Although there is nothing wrong with altering a recipe to suit your own preferences, make the dish as directed the first time you try a recipe. You might think your substitutions will be as good as the original, but do you really want to risk culinary disaster at a party?

If you are a novice chef, try preparing the recipes ahead of time for a much smaller group. You'll get an idea of potential pitfalls involved with making each dish, and you will have practiced making the dishes so that your guests will not suffer from your inexperience with cooking.

If you are an experienced cook, tried-and-true recipes are still the best choice for a party. If you want to make something new and have never cooked anything similar before, plan a practice dinner. Parties are not the time to try out brand-new recipes.

I do need to think about the actual cooking time because more than one dish utilizes the oven.

After the pork slow-cooks all night, it needs to boil for 45 minutes. The roast needs to go in the oven at 350 degrees for a total of 1½ hours. The bean dip needs to bake at 350 degrees until the dish is warmed and the cheese melts, about 15 minutes at most. Because I'll need to remove the pork from the oven halfway through the cooking time to ladle broth over it and turn it, I'll pop the bean dip in during that time, remove, and serve it when the cheese melts, and then put the pork back in for another 45 minutes. The dip, which I'm serving as an appetizer, will be ready to go at about 4:30, soon after my guests arrive. Perfect timing!

The beverages will be prepared to order, so all I'll need to do is have a pitcher of margaritas ready to go at 4:00 p.m., when the first guests arrive. I will need to remember to put all the beer, soda, and water in the refrigerator the night before, so they are already chilled when I stick them in the ice bucket the next day.

Okay, I think that's everything!

Finalizing the List

I can now add the specific food preparation steps to my to-do list and sort the list by when everything needs to be done. I can also review my planned tasks and see if I need to revise my list: I might have to do some things even further ahead of time.

caution   I lucked out! Both my oven dishes utilize the same cooking temperature. However, I'm not always this lucky. Oftentimes, dishes will require different oven temperatures. Check your recipes carefully ahead of time to determine in what order you'll need to cook them. If you can, cook the dish with the lowest oven temperature first, and then turn up the heat for the rest of your cooking. If you simply cannot do this (a fresh dessert that needs to be baked at a lower temperature, for example), reduce the temperature, open the oven door, and allow the oven to cool to your desired temperature. To ensure you're cooking at the right heat, purchase an inexpensive oven thermometer, which can be found at any housewares store.

note   A few days before the party, take a few minutes to clean out your refrigerator and freezer, tossing any old or expired food. After your shopping trips, you'll need every inch of space to store your party ingredients. There's nothing worse than realizing on party day that your prepared dishes just won't fit!

Task	Month Before	Week Before	Two Days Before	Day Before	Party Day
Send out invitations	X				
Visit Mexican market		X			
Check propane and clean grill		X			
Get items on "I'll Need" list		X			
Clean bathroom		X			
Clean kitchen		X			
Launder clothing		X			
Tidy yards		X			
Dust and tidy house		X			
Visit Smart & Final		X			
Clean out fridge		X			
Select party CDs		X			
Visit Trader Joe's			X		
Visit Costco			X		
Visit party store				X	
Visit grocery store				X	
Launder rugs				X	
Change cat litter box				X	
Chop vegetables and prepare garnishes				X	
Prepare pork and begin slow cooking				X	
Bake brownies				X	
Refrigerate beverages				X	
Sweep floors					X
Empty trash and recycling					X
Pick up dog deposits					X
Clean patio furniture					X
Move stereo					X
Make guacamole					X
Ready bean dip, chips, and salsa					X
Decorate party areas					X

continues

Task	Month Before	Week Before	Two Days Before	Day Before	Party Day
Stew pork					X
Feed and walk dogs					X
Get myself ready for the party					X
Begin baking pork					X
Prepare pitcher of margaritas					X
Bake bean dip					X
Cook tilapia					X
Arrange tortillas and garnishes in serving dishes					X
Finish baking pork					X
Serve dinner					X

As I thought, cleaning the house, buying the fresh ingredients, and preparing the ahead-of-time food is too much work for the night before the party. I'll revise my plan so that I clean the house during the week before, and then, just before the party, touch up anything that gets dirty.

For the sake of your guests' health, your food-preparation and serving areas *must* be clean. Spray down countertops and anywhere else you are preparing and serving food with disinfecting spray and wipe thoroughly. Also, as you are cutting meat and vegetables, use separate cutting surfaces. A wooden cutting board or butcher's block is fine for everything but meat, which must be cut on a nonporous surface, such as plastic. Be sure to disinfect your meat-cutting surface before you cut each type of meat; for example, I'll cut up the pork, and then wipe down the board before I prepare the fish.

Now that I've listed all the tasks I'll need to do, I can itemize everything and create a schedule that works for me.

Before I get started, I'll look at my existing calendar and see if I have any appointments or deadlines that might interfere with any of these tasks, and then adjust my party schedule accordingly. For example, in the week before the party, I have a dinner date on Tuesday night, so I'll make sure I don't need to do anything party-related that night.

Okay, let's turn that clever little chart into a schedule!

CLEANING HOUSE

Although you might prefer to offer a gleaming, freshly cleaned house to your guests, sometimes it's just not practical.

If you have a lot to do the day before the party and find yourself wondering when you'll get everything done, clean the house up to a week ahead of time, scrubbing the bathroom, kitchen, and any areas within the house where you expect guests to linger. The day of the party, simply touch up any spills or smudges, especially in the bathroom, with any of the premoistened cleaning wipes on the market.

If you're really strapped for time, focus on cleaning the *visible* dirt. If you simply have no time for a top-to-bottom spring cleaning, at least give the illusion of having cleaned, taking care of hot spots in your home:

* Banish clutter. Throw away junk mail, stack unsorted mail and paperwork on your desk or out of sight, clear all counters and table tops, and pick everything up from the floor.

* Sweep or vacuum the floors. Mop if you have time; use a cleaning wipe to remove visible dirt if you cannot mop.

* Spray the kitchen countertops with all-purpose cleaner and wipe down quickly. Use a cleaning wipe to remove any spills from the cabinets and stove.

* Attack the bathroom with cleaning wipes, quickly swiping mirrors, chrome, countertops, and the toilet. Make sure the porcelain base and tank are free of dirt.

* Sweep your front porch and/or walkway.

If you can manage only 15 minutes of cleaning before the party (it happens!), focus on areas that *must* appear clean: kitchen counters, the bathroom countertops and toilet, and the entryway, which will be your guests' first impression of your home.

Scheduling Your Time

Because I now have a list of everything that needs to be accomplished before the party date, my next step is to schedule out each task, adding dates and times to the to-do list, which will help me stay organized and focused. I can also take a look at what I'll need to do each date; estimate how much time it will take, if necessary; and plan each task in the order I will need to accomplish it. By doing all this, I will eliminate stress before I even begin to feel it, ensuring I'm rested and energized the day of the party.

Here's my schedule:

Month Ahead

Send out invitations	1 hour

Saturday (4/27)

Visit Mexican market	1 hour
Get together items on "I'll Need" list	2 hours

Sunday (4/28)

Check propane and clean grill	1 hour
Tidy yards	3 hours

Monday (4/29)

Visit Smart & Final	30 minutes
Clean out fridge	30 minutes

Wednesday (5/1)

Launder clothing	All night
Clean bathroom	30 minutes
Clean kitchen	30 minutes
Dust and tidy house	1 hour

Thursday (5/2)

Visit Trader Joe's	1 hour
Visit Costco	1 hour

Friday (5/3)

Visit party store	15 minutes
Visit grocery store	30 minutes
Launder rugs	All night
Change cat litter box	15 minutes
Refrigerate beverages	15 minutes
Bake brownies	1 hour
Chop vegetables and prepare garnishes	1 hour
Prepare pork and begin slow cooking	30 minutes

Saturday (5/4): Party Day!

Wake up and eat breakfast	9:00
Empty trash and recycling	10:30
Pick up dog deposits	10:45
Clean patio furniture	11:00
Decorate party areas	11:15
Set out favors	12:30
Sweep floors	12:45
Move stereo	1:00
Select party CDs	1:00
Walk dogs	1:15
Stew pork (simmer until ready to bake)	1:45
Get myself ready for the party	2:00
Begin baking pork	3:15
Make guacamole	3:15
Arrange tortillas/garnishes in serving dishes	3:30
Ready bean dip, chips, and salsa	3:30
Ready for guests to arrive!	3:30
Bake bean dip	4:00
Prepare pitcher of margaritas	4:00
Finish baking pork	4:30
Cook tilapia	5:00
Grill vegetables	5:15
Serve dinner	5:30

If you find that scheduling your party-day tasks makes your head spin, start at the end and work your way backward. Leave enough time for each task to take a little more time than you'd planned. Also, leave time for emergencies. If you are very new to party-giving, leave more time. If you are a pro, leave as much time as you think you'll need, a minimum of one extra hour.

Now that I have scheduled everything into manageable tasks, I can take a deep breath, relax, and put party planning behind me, confident that I've thought of everything and anticipated anything that could go wrong. Perhaps a round of drinks might be in order?

Summary

In this chapter, we looked at our shopping list and tasks, turning a long, disparate list of to-do items into an easily managed list of activities. I know what to buy, where to buy it, how to prepare it, and when to do so, scheduling every task down to the minute. In the next chapter, we'll take a closer look at the day of the party, walking through every minute of the big day and making sure we are ready for the event. We'll do our best to get everything done quickly, eliminating stress before it has a chance to affect us. We'll virtually attend the party, looking at what should happen when—and what to do if it doesn't!

tip As you get ready the day of the party, wear clothing with pockets, where you can stow your portable house phone and/or cell phone. You are going to get a number of calls the day of the party, people RSVPing at the last minute and wanting to know what to wear. Please do delegate any last-minute grocery-store items to your thoughtful guests who ask if you need anything—people like to help!

7

The Big Day: Successfully Hosting a Party

In the last two chapters, we did a lot of planning. In this chapter, we'll put all that planning to the test as we throw ourselves a Cinco de Mayo Fiesta. I'll be your virtual guide to this party, showing how our planning translates into a party our guests won't forget. We'll make sure we've accomplished all the pre-party tasks before the guests arrive, and then ensure the party runs smoothly by monitoring the flow of conversation; keeping the food, drinks, and activities on-track; and ending the evening gracefully.

Hopefully, all will go well, but if something does go wrong, we'll handle it. How? With grace and tact, of course!

To do list

- [ ] Review your task list and determine what's left to do before the guests arrive
- [ ] Handle any emergencies, including items you forgot to purchase or loaner items you weren't able to find
- [ ] Take "snapshots" of your planning and make sure you are ready to go

Checking the Status of Your Party Preparations

As the party hour nears, we'll need to make the most of our time. By using our task list as a strict guide, we'll stay focused, keeping just busy enough that we won't have time to worry about anything. Just in case emergencies do arise, we'll try to handle them without feeling frazzled.

You'll Need

❑ The Task List we created in Chapter 6, "Counting Down"

❑ The "You'll Need" list we created in Chapter 5, "Planning Ahead"

Reviewing Your Task List

Check that checklist, baby! By the day of the party, we should have completed everything on our task list, except for those things we left to the day of the party. To review, here's what we need to get accomplished before our guests arrive later today:

Wake up and eat breakfast	9:00
~~Empty trash and recycling~~	~~10:00~~
Pick up dog deposits	10:30
~~Clean patio furniture~~	~~10:45~~
Decorate party areas	11:00
Sweep floors	12:00
Move stereo, set out favors	12:15
Walk dogs	12:30
Stew pork (simmer until ready to bake)	1:00
Make guacamole	1:15
Take mental snapshots of your party arena	1:30
Get myself ready for the party	1:45
Begin baking pork	2:45
Lay out buffet table with plates, utensils, serving dishes bean dip, chips, and salsa, tortillas and garnishes	3:00

Get mentally ready for guests to arrive!	3:30
Bake bean dip	4:00
Prepare pitcher of margaritas	4:00
Finish baking pork	4:30
Cook tilapia	5:00
Grill vegetables	5:15
Serve dinner	5:30

Before we start our pre-party work, let's review everything on our list—perhaps over a lovely cup of coffee? Because we have almost every minute planned today, we want to make sure we keep on track. Although there is plenty of time to get everything done, we don't want anyone feeling overwhelmed.

If you feel your head spinning when you begin thinking about all you need to do to get ready for your party, sit down, take a deep breath, and look at the list. If you stick with your schedule, you'll get everything done in plenty of time to enjoy a great party.

I cleaned off the patio furniture a few days ago and took out the trash and recycling last night, so I've already crossed those items off my list. It's a good thing, too, because I completely forgot to go to the party store yesterday for balloons!

Handling Any Emergencies

Emergencies are going to arise—it's a fact of life. Although we have taken great measures to ensure we get as much done ahead of time as possible, we are, after all, humans, and humans forget things. Try not to castigate yourself; just stay calm and think the problem through. There *is* a solution to every problem.

I thought I was ahead of the game because I took care of a couple "party day" chores prior to the big day. However, I was so busy cleaning, shopping, and preparing the food that I forgot I was supposed to go to the party store yesterday and get the helium balloons!

I have about 30 minutes to take care of this minor emergency, which is plenty of time because the party store is just four blocks away. I'll kill two birds with my party-store trip and take the dogs with me. They'll enjoy the walk, and the party store welcomes leashed pets.

After I get to the store, I realize I have another emergency—the balloons cost way more than I thought they would! Although the party store is having a special on Mylar balloons (a bunch of five for $5.99), I don't like the goofy ones available. Regular balloons—in red, white, and green—can be filled with helium and will look great, but they'll cost $12, way more than the $5 I have budgeted. It's time to bust out the emergency fund. I hate dipping into it, but that's what it's for, right? Emergencies!

While I was shopping for groceries, I was able to get a few items at discount stores for a lower price than I thought. I'd put the extra money in my emergency fund, without even looking to see how much I'd accumulated.

Now, at the party store, I'm relieved to find that I have almost $50 in the emergency fund. Not only can I get the balloons I want, but I can also stop at Costco on the way home and pick up that bottle of premium tequila I was hoping to add to the beverage buffet.

There's only one problem: If I run to Costco, I'll need to add another half-hour errand to my schedule. Even if I find a good parking spot and run straight for the liquor aisle, it's going to take at least twenty minutes to wait in line and check out.

Looking over my list, I'm going to need some help if I want to get everything done in time—oh, wait! I already walked the dogs to and from the party store, so I can cross that task off my list. Problem solved!

note Whenever possible, multi-task. As in my party store/dog walking example, I was able to save much-needed time by combining activities. Your schedule will, of course, vary, but you'll probably be able to find a few activities you can take care of at once, such as watering the yard while you're cleaning the patio, doing laundry while you're preparing the food, cleaning house while you're waiting for do-ahead items to marinate or cook, or making last-minute phone calls while you're answering your email. Be creative, and you'll find all sorts of ways to cut time from your budget, minutes you might find will come in handy while you're racing around at the last minute.

As you find your own emergencies arising, try not to let them affect your good mood. Remember that you'll need to greet your guests with a happy face if you don't want them to turn tail and flee, so take a deep breath, deal with your emergencies—ask friends for help if you need it—and *don't freak out*. It's *your* party, yes, but it is just a party. Your guests won't think less of you if a couple of tasks remain unfinished. Just do your best, and have fun!

Taking "Snapshots" of Your Party Planning

After you've completed all the pre-party tasks leading up to your hour of "me" time, take a few minutes to survey your home. These "snapshots" will accomplish two goals: You can double-check your task list and make sure you've completed all your party assignments, and you'll give yourself a little boost as you force yourself to take note of all the wonderful preparations you've made.

It's 2:00 p.m., and I'm just about to jump in the shower for a long, hot, pre-party soak. Before I do so, I'll take mental snapshots of the party arena, just to make sure everything is really ready to go. I'll compile my mental photograph album based on the initial budget and task lists I made previously.

Reviewing Your Budget

Take a peek into your envelopes and see how much money you have left. Anything you haven't spent should go into the emergency fund. If you have a few dollars left, you've done a great job. If all your envelopes are empty, you've spent your money wisely. If you used your credit card to make up the difference between what you budgeted and what you actually spent, then you know what to do differently next time.

Even with the expensive balloons and extra bottle of tequila, I have $5 left. Not quite enough for a plane ticket to Hawaii, but that $5 will go into my little envelope for my next party. When you give as many parties as I do, every penny counts!

What I'm really happy about, though, is that I spent close to my entire budget, almost exactly as I'd planned. It's great to save money, but because I didn't scrimp too much, my guests will enjoy delicious food and beverages in a setting that's clean, festive, and appropriately decorated—and we'll all enjoy a few shots from the sweet bottle of tequila I picked up at Costco.

Eyeballing the Venue

Just before you jump in the shower, take a moment to look around your home. Everything should be clean and orderly, with clutter stowed and no visible dirt anywhere, including the floors. The yard and entryway should be swept—check to make sure you remembered to put the broom away! This is your last chance to take a good look around, so make it a good, long look.

I did little bits of cleaning all week long—it's spring, so I went a little overboard. Although I'm tired, my house looks great. The bathroom and kitchen are sparkling, from chrome to porcelain; the floors are swept; the couches are free of dog hair and lint; everything is organized, tidy, and put away; and I even found time to sweep the baseboards!

Taking one last look, I'll make sure the toilet-paper and paper-towel dispensers are filled, with replacement rolls nearby. After I take my shower and get ready, I'll wipe off the mirror and chrome fixtures in the bathroom. Finally, I'll take one last look around to make sure everything looks the way it's supposed to—ready for a party.

Taking a Last Look at the Guest List

Even though most guests have good intentions, sometimes people can't RSVP until the very last minute. If you used Evite or another web-based RSVP system, take a quick look to see if your numbers have changed. Although there isn't a lot you can do about it now, you'll still want to know who can and can't make it. Make sure you check your email and phone messages, too.

A quick trip online will tell me the status of my guest list. Because I used Evite, my guests were able to RSVP online, some at the very last minute. I'm happy to see that almost everyone is coming. It looks like I'll have about 50 guests, which is just right for the amount of food and beverages I purchased.

Forestalling Food Worries

Because food preparation is usually the most extensive item on your task list, chances are good that it's also the element you're the most stressed out about. As you look over your food preparations, give yourself a pat on the back—if you stuck to the schedule, everything is ready to go. Except for a few things that can't be prepared until just before serving, your food should be delectably ready to eat.

I was able to prepare much of the food ahead of time, and I just have a few more food-related tasks to finish before the guests arrive at 4:00 p.m.: Bake the pork; heat the bean dip; arrange the chips, salsa, tortillas, and garnishes on the buffet table; and make the guacamole. I'll need to fry the fish and grill the vegetables after the guests arrive, but the ingredients and necessary tools are ready to go. So far, so good.

I've been careful to ensure any food that might spoil has been covered and will remain refrigerated until ready to serve. If you have any of those cute little inverted baskets that keep flies from landing on food, feel free to set out your garnishes or chips up to an hour before the guests arrive, as long as none of the ingredients need to be kept cold, such as in the case of sour cream–based dips or lettuce, which can wilt.

Double-Checking the Drinks

If you remembered to chill your cold drinks the night before, you're practically good to go. Just make sure you have enough ice, and you're all set.

I put the soda, water, and beer in the fridge last night, before I went to bed, so they are chilled and ready for the ice buckets. I'll ice them at 3:30, just before the guests arrive, and then make that pitcher of margaritas to get things started.

Tracking Your Tools

Although it might seem prudent to lay out your eating and serving utensils now, before you shower, wait a little longer. If you set out everything too early, you run the risk of having the wind blow stuff around or a bird depositing his own very special hostess gift on your buffet table. At this point, your cups, plates, utensils, serving dishes, serving utensils, and napkins should be stacked on an inside table, ready to set out on the buffet table after your shower and before your guests arrive.

As you are laying out the tools for the buffet or serving table, do yourself a favor and determine how many serving utensils you'll need for your different dishes. You'll want one large spoon for each dish served in a bowl; a meat fork for each meat plate; a fork for each garnish plate (lettuce, tomato, and onion slices); a ladle if you're serving punch, gravy, or salad dressing from a dish; a butter knife; and knives or spoons for any relishes or condiments. Before you even bring out the food, have these implements ready on the table so that all you'll have to do is place them in or next to their corresponding serving dish.

The buffet table is covered and ready to be loaded down with food and tools, the cups, plates, utensils, serving dishes, serving utensils, and napkins are stacked on the washing machine, and I have a trashcan set out for debris.

I've also placed extra bag liners in the bottom of the trashcan and recycling bin, under the liners I'm currently using. When the bags are full, I can lift out the used liner, sweetly ask my husband to take it to the big can in the side yard, and quickly line the can with a fresh bag.

> **tip**
> Make a little "Recyclables Only" sign for your extra trashcan, so guests will know what to do with their empty bottles and cans. Even if you don't recycle (shame on you!), you might want to utilize this tip—otherwise, you'll have to answer "just put that in the trashcan" about 106 times throughout the night, as each guest wants to know where to stow their empties.

Surveying Your Décor

Now is when you'll get the chance to really be proud of yourself—looking over your décor and enjoying the tingly feeling of knowing you've created a well-dressed party venue. Also take a moment to make sure you didn't leave anything out, such as tape, trash bags, scissors, or any other tools you used to spiff up the place.

I'm fairly proud of my décor—I didn't have much money to spend, but my backyard looks very "Cinco de Maya Fiesta." I tied the balloons to the fence in a couple of small clumps, spread out the Mexican blankets in a few areas at the edge of the lawn, arranged the sombreros in key spots, and covered the picnic and buffet tables with some bright-red tablecloths, holding down the edges with the saints candles I've been accumulating. I've even set out a few ashtrays for smokers.

The tiki torches are filled with oil and staked in appropriate areas around the backyard. I've placed white tapers, columns, and votives around the house, stowing matches nearby. I won't light the tiki torches or candles until it gets dark, because I don't want to have to monitor the open flames until it's absolutely necessary. However, I will light a candle in the bathroom—the candle is safely enclosed in glass, and the sweet scent of lavender will make my guests more comfortable.

Assessing Activities

If you've planned any activities for your party, take a few minutes to make sure you have everything you need, set out and ready to go. You will have already checked your games for missing pieces and dice; just make sure the games or activities are displayed on the coffee or side table, tempting guests with their zany packaging.

Also think of any last-minute planning you might need to do for your activities. Are you sure of the rules? Do you know when you'll be undertaking these activities? If you're offering prizes, did you remember to wrap them or stick a festive bow on them?

I have two planned activities—the beer tasting and the piñata pummeling. I'm not planning a very structured party, but I do need to consider dinner, which will be ready at 5:30 p.m. I'd planned the beer tasting for 6:00 p.m., which should work out well. People will have eaten a little bit by then, so they won't be guzzling beer on an empty stomach.

I've also acquired a prize for the tasting—an extra sombrero my friend, Tony, doesn't want back. Because this isn't really a contest, I'll have to wing it. The sombrero will either go to the person who brought the best beer or to the taster who does the best job. It's highly subjective, but I don't think it will matter. The sombrero is ghastly, so it's really a joke gift, anyway.

I'd planned to do the piñata a while later, at about 8:00 p.m., when the party mellows. If hitting a candy-filled paper-mache goat with large sticks doesn't liven up the party, nothing will! I've already hung the piñata from a tree in the backyard, and I've lined up a baseball bat.

I'm going to remember to begin these two activities at what seems like natural times during the party. If the beer tasting doesn't happen until 7:00 p.m., there's no reason to get upset. Likewise with the piñata—even if that activity doesn't take place until after dark, I'm not going to stress myself out about it. The lighting will be fine!

Monitoring the Music

Your CDs should be stacked by the stereo, with the first CD loaded into the player. Check the batteries in the remote, and set it by the clothing you'll wear.

I've gone through my CDs and picked out a bunch I think will be great for the party. I've even loaded Pink Martini's *Sympatique* (I begin every party, regardless of theme, with this CD) into the player, and moved the stereo to where it can be heard inside and outside the house.

tip As I've mentioned a few times, I'll keep the stereo remote (with fresh batteries!) in my pocket during the party. That way, I can adjust the volume easily, even if I'm in the middle of a conversation.

Finalizing Your Favors

You've saved the easiest task for last: Checking on your favors will only take a second. Make sure they are festively displayed in a bowl or other presentation dish near the front door, on the picnic table, or another spot where guests will be likely to linger. That's it!

I had a ball at the Mexican market, picking out all sorts of little toys for party favors. I've already arranged them in a bowl, which I set in the foyer next to a sign reading "Celebrate Cinco de Mayo!" After everyone arrives and dinner is over, I'll move the bowl to the picnic table so that guests can play with the toys left in the bowl.

Now that I've made sure all my different elements are ready for the party, I'm off to the shower, where I will relax and mentally prepare myself for the hard work and good fun that's about to happen.

When I'm physically ready for the party, I'll throw on an apron and hop into the kitchen to take care of all my last-minute food-related preparations. I'll appear ready and organized, even if a few helpful souls arrive frighteningly early.

caution Make sure you don't lose **track of time while you're getting ready!** Although one goal of a long, hot shower (or bath) is to mentally prepare you for the party, you will only stress yourself out further if you spend too long in the tub. If you don't already have a clock in the bathroom, take in a timepiece and consult it frequently enough to keep yourself on schedule.

Managing Your Party's Progression

Now we're down to the nitty gritty: The guests are about to arrive, and all your careful preparations will pay off with a fabulous party your guests will love.

Although you've done most of the real work, don't rest on your laurels for too long, lest your party fizzles or becomes unmanageable. With a few gentle reminders and an attentive eye, you'll have a great time, even as you're making sure your guests enjoy themselves.

To do list

- ❏ Greet your guests warmly, no matter what time they arrive
- ❏ Serve dinner and beverages
- ❏ Execute planned activities
- ❏ Monitor the flow of your party
- ❏ Close down shop and tactfully encourage guests to leave as the hour grows late

Remembering Your Manners

In Chapter 4, "Minding Your Ps and Qs," you learned how to be a well-mannered host. It's time to put your training to good use as you welcome your guests. As a reminder, when each person arrives, do the following:

- Open the door with a smile on your face.
- Make sure you know the guests' names: "Hi, you must be [insert name of housemate]'s friends. I don't think we've met." You will need this information later in the party, when you are introducing these guests to other people. Try to create an instant mnemonic device for remembering names: "Patty's Purse is Pink" or something equally silly and memorable.
- Ask to take coats and bags, or direct guests to an appropriate spot where they can stash their things, such as on a bed in a room with a closed door.
- Escort your guests to the food or beverage table, or ensure they have a place to roost comfortably.

By taking a few moments with each guest, you will begin the event with everyone feeling welcomed and appreciated. Although you aren't required to have a sit-down with guests as they arrive, you should make sure you spend at least five or ten minutes at some point in the party talking one-on-one with each guest or group of guests.

In addition to greeting guests, don't forget the following polite behaviors:

- Introduce guests to one another, remembering to use each guest's name twice ("Bob, this is Shirley; Shirley, Bob"), supply a frame of reference for how you know each guest, and offer an interesting fact about which they might converse.

TACTFUL DELEGATION

Just because you are the host, it doesn't mean you have to do every last bit of work, especially if early-arriving guests offer a hand.

Although Miss Manners would not approve of actually planning to hand tasks to guests as they arrive, there is nothing wrong with answering an offer of help with a pleasant, "Why, yes! I could really use your help with…"

Here are a couple of pointers for delegating tasks:

* Try not to ask someone to do something unless she first offers help. You can suspend this rule if the guest is your best friend or close relative.

* Don't ask your guests to do anything that might cause them to sweat, ruin their attire, or hurt themselves. Leave the heavy lifting for the brawny guys, and let your petite friend Michelle arrange the garnish plate.

* Don't micromanage. Allow your helpers to perform the task according to their abilities. If that means surreptitiously making a few discreet adjustments—or simply being satisfied with a job you didn't have to do—then so be it.

* Show gratitude. As the party gets going, thank your guests for their help. As a nice touch, send them a little after-party thank-you email, as well.

Transferring the refrigerated beverages to the outdoor ice buckets is a perfect task for delegation—it's easy, doesn't require any heavy lifting, and won't mess up my guests' clothing. Also, it isn't particularly difficult, and the world won't end if I wind up doing this task myself.

You might also delegate arranging the garnishes, carrying out to the table the chips and dips, lighting the candles and tiki torches at dusk, and "judging" the beer tasting.

* Remember to use good manners while serving, drinking, and eating, with the hope that your other guests will follow the example you set.

* Keep the conversation flowing with appropriate comments, anecdotes, and questions—no politics, religion, or gossip!

* Gently inform your guests of the house rules ("No smoking in the house, please!"), and diplomatically enforce them.

* Don't get drunk! Although you can imbibe if you choose, limit your drinks to one per hour. You are the hostess, and you will need to keep your head about you for the duration of your party. You can polish off the margaritas *after* the guests leave.

If you practice these basic rules of etiquette, you will set the tone for the party, guiding your guests toward good conduct. If you do encounter any rude or unwanted behavior, remove the offender in a tactful, gracious manner, and have a private place for a little talk, if necessary.

Serving Up Food and Drink

While your guests are chatting, drinking, and eating the appetizers, flit back to the kitchen to take care of the last-minute food preparation. At my party, for example, I'll toss the bean dip into the oven and remove it when it's warm, put the pork pan into the waiting oven, fry the fish, and grill the vegetables.

As you take care of these simple tasks, chat with anyone who ventures into the kitchen. At the beginning of the party, when few guests are present, many people will congregate in the kitchen, making it easy for you to entertain as you cook.

If your early guests ask if they can help, give them a small, simple task (see the "Tactful Delegation" sidebar). Most men enjoy grilling, which gives them a little job to do while quaffing beer and waiting for more people to arrive. You might also enlist offered help with the fish frying, which is really easy and will make your helpers feel as though they played a major role in the dinner preparations.

If you feel stressed out, trying to cook and chat at the same time, just take a deep breath and try to relax. At this point, entertaining your guests is more important than fixing the food. If dinner is a little later than you'd planned, no one will mind. Remember, your schedule is for your eyes only. If the dinner is served a half-hour late, who will know?

Because this party is a buffet, we won't have to worry too much about actually serving guests their food. By 5:30, an hour and a half into the party, the fish should be fried, the vegetables grilled, and the pork dished onto a serving platter. All we'll need to do is carry everything out to the buffet table and announce that dinner is served.

You will need to give a little thought to how you'll lay out your table. Because both entrees—carnitas and tilapia tacos—require assembly, arrange the different dishes in a logical order: tortillas, cabbage, cheese, onion, guacamole, salsa, bean dip, sour cream, avocado slices, limes, cilantro, grilled vegetables, and meat.

caution

Even if you don't think you'll have any vegetarians present, respect the eating practice by segregating the food: vegetables, tortillas, salsa, and dips in one area, and meat and fish at the end of the table. Also, ensure your grill is clean before you grill the vegetables, so your vegetarian guests won't have to wonder if their entree is being cooked atop meat remnants.

Make certain your plates, eating utensils, and napkins are at the left of the table, where guests will begin lining up, and your tortillas, garnishes, vegetables, and meats move from left to right. You can either set out the brownies at this time or save them for later, after guests have digested their dinner.

Expect your guests to arrange their food in any manner they choose. Some might build soft-tortilla tostadas, whereas others might make small burritos. One of the benefits to this type of meal is that people can choose exactly what they want, in their desired quantity and combination.

Finally, the rule about the hostess taking the first bite doesn't really apply to a buffet setting. You will probably still be carrying out dishes as your guests begin to load their plates. However, if your guests seem reluctant to approach the table, do them a favor by showing them how it's done: Grab a plate, a napkin, and your eating utensils, and create a gorgeous taco or two. You'll accomplish two tasks—leading the crowd to the food and showing anyone unfamiliar with these Mexican dishes exactly how they are assembled.

After each guest has had his or her fill, going back for seconds—or even thirds!—tidy up the buffet table. Dispose of any trash, clean up any messes, and cover dishes so they aren't exposed to bugs. If everyone seems genuinely stuffed to his maximum capacity, return food to the kitchen, refrigerating anything that might spoil, such as the meat, cheese, or sour cream.

After the table is set to rights, take inventory of your beverage stock. If you need to bring out more soda, beer, or water, do so now. Likewise, your margarita supply might need replenishing.

Monitoring the Flow

Because this fiesta is a casual, backyard buffet, the normal rules of mingling don't apply as stringently as they would at a cocktail or dinner party. Allow guests to gather into small groups at the picnic table or on the Mexican blankets, eating, drinking, and conversing as they please, and don't feel compelled to "work the yard."

However, you will want to monitor the flow of your party, just to ensure that everyone is having a great time, that no one is uncomfortable, and that your evening is progressing as you've planned. Here's a rough guideline of what should be happening as the hours drift by:

- **4:00 p.m.**—Guests arrive, sample chips and dips, get drinks, and chat with one another.

- **5:00 p.m.**—As guests continue to nosh and mingle, you'll be frying the fish, readying the pork, and arranging food in serving dishes.

- **5:30 p.m.**—Dinner is served!

- **6:30 p.m.**—Begin the beer-tasting activity.

- **8:00 p.m.**—Begin the piñata bashing!

- **9:00 p.m.**—Serve dessert (if you didn't already set out the brownies); continue to encourage your guests to drink and mingle. Feel free to sit down and rest for a few minutes. Expect that some guests will begin to leave; if the party is still lively, consider busting out the premium tequila and pouring a few shots.

- **10:00 p.m.**—More guests will leave; those who remain will continue drinking. Make and serve coffee.

- **11:00 p.m.**—Most guests will have left by this point. Any who remain will be doing so at their own risk—you are now free to drink, should you feel so inclined.

Although this schedule is likely to fluctuate, you'll be prepared if you have an idea of what should occur when. Don't hold to the schedule, checking your watch every few minutes to ensure your party is on time. Let the activity flow as it naturally occurs, being careful that no guests are stranded and that conversation is thriving.

Entertaining with Activities

Mexican Beer Tasting

When the time is right, assess the beer supply and determine how the tasting should proceed. For this event, select up to ten different bottles of beer, depending upon who brought what, and pour three small tastes of each. Ask for three volunteers to perform the tasting.

Introduce each beer—or ask the person who brought it to do the honors. After blindfolding the volunteers, give each person a taste of beer and ask them to guess which beer they're drinking. Whoever guesses the most tastes correctly "wins" the hideous sombrero.

Piñata Bashing

I know this activity will be a smash—who doesn't love hitting things with impunity? As the time nears for the piñata bashing, I'll check the rope, ensuring it's looped over a tree branch in a way that allows the piñata to be raised and lowered without slipping down the tree branch. When the time is right, I'll announce that the bashing can commence.

Be aware that you are asking blindfolded, potentially intoxicated guests to arm themselves with a baseball bat and strike a moving target. Remember a few safety rules:

- If people don't want to participate, don't goad them on. Let people dictate what activities they can and cannot safely undertake.

- Only allow one person at a time to strike the piñata, and keep the other guests safely out of striking range.

- After each guest has three tries at striking the piñata, have him surrender the bat to the next person.

If no one is able to successfully break the piñata, lower it to the ground and have a ceremonial breaking by allowing the silliest guest to attack the piñata. Stand back as your guests rush the candy and toys like six-year-olds on Halloween.

Closing Down Shop

As guests begin to leave, put your best hostess face back on and give each departing person a cheerful good-bye, thanking them for attending. Show each guest to the door, helping them find any coats or purses they stowed.

As the hour grows late and your party starts to wind down, make two pots of coffee, one regular and one decaf, and be sure to mark the pots so guests will know what they are drinking. Arrange the coffee pots on the buffet table, along with cream, sweetener, sugar, and any nifty accoutrements you might have, such as cinnamon, whipped cream, vanilla syrup, or cocoa. Announce that the coffee is ready for anyone who wants it.

> **caution** **Don't make guests feel guilty for making an early exit!** Most people have busy lives, and no matter how much they have enjoyed the party, there are often children, pets, or other responsibilities waiting for them at home.

As noted previously, coffee is nature's miracle, alerting guests with its rich smell that it's time to pack it in and go home. As such, don't make the coffee until the party starts to flag, or until you do!

After everyone has left, take care of those cleanup tasks that can't wait until morning, such as cleaning up all the food, the buffet table, the grill, and anywhere guests were eating or drinking. Dispose of all trash, including empty bottles and cups, and take the bags out. Taking a half hour to put away these few things will ensure you aren't visited by bugs or other pests intent on enjoying your guests' leavings.

If you have the energy and dedication, clean up the whole mess. However, by now, you will very likely be ready for bed. Don't feel at all bad about leaving the rest of the mess for the next day.

Summary

In this chapter, you learned how to take care of last-minute tasks, emergencies, and delegation of duties. You greeted your guests, fed and watered them, entertained them, and made sure they had a great time, bidding them farewell and thanking them as they left. After you've hosted your party, it's time to deal with the aftermath—cleaning up after your guests. You learn more about that process in Chapter 8, "The After Party."

The After Party

8

The party's over / it's time to call it a day.... I sing this Jule Styne song every time I say goodbye to the last guests, sadly closing the door behind them. I am sad not because the party is over, however, but because now I must clean up the mess.

Fortunately, time and experience have taught me the fastest, least painful method for dealing with party debris. In this chapter, I'll share that knowledge with you, and offer a few words about what to do with the leftover food, should there be any. I'll also give you a few tips for thanking those guests who brought you gifts or helped you with the party.

You'll Need

- ❏ Plastic food-storage containers with lids
- ❏ Plastic wrap
- ❏ Aluminum foil
- ❏ Ziploc bags
- ❏ Garbage bags
- ❏ Recycle bin
- ❏ Bucket

In this chapter:

- ✳ Learn how to deal with leftovers—what can be saved and what must be tossed
- ✳ Discover the fastest, easiest way to clean up the mess your guests have left behind
- ✳ Understand the importance of following up with your guests after the party

Mandatory Cleaning

Before you go to bed, you absolutely *must* clean up any leftover food. Even if you aren't interested in reheating today's tilapia tomorrow, the last thing you want to wake up to is a plate full of stinky, gross fish bits. Likewise, you'll want to dispose of any bottles, cans, and half-filled plastic cups, lest you be the target of an early morning ant attack.

As you survey the mess in your kitchen and backyard, try not to feel discouraged. Put on a soothing (or invigorating!) CD and take things one step at a time. You'll clean up that mess in no time, and be off to bed, having dealt with the bare minimum before your head hits the pillow.

To do list

- ❑ Safely store anything edible
- ❑ Do the bare-minimum amount of cleanup before bed

Safely Storing Leftovers

Begin your cleanup efforts with the food. Earlier in the evening, you were to have brought in anything that wasn't consumed during the buffet and stored it in the fridge if it needed to be kept cold. It's likely that everything else is moldering on your once-clean serving platters, looking bulky and unmanageable.

Grab a serving tray and head out to the yard, piling on the tray any serving dishes still remaining on the buffet. Empty the tray and hit the living room or any other area in which you laid out food or drink. After you've relocated all your serving dishes, platters, bowls, pitchers, and utensils to the kitchen, you are ready to begin storing the food.

Start your food cleanup by throwing away anything that has spoiled or isn't worth saving. Grab a trash bag, and toss chips that have become stale, dips that have sat out too long, any meat or dairy products that didn't make it to the fridge, or anything that was used as an ashtray. Shake uneaten food off the paper plates and into the garbage, and pour unfinished drinks down the drain.

As you get rid of your uneaten inedibles, stack the serving dishes and utensils in the sink. Anything made of paper, plastic, or aluminum should be thrown in a separate bag for recycling—just make sure your recyclables are free of food and drink.

Next, tackle the food you want to save. Because you've thrown out everything that won't live to see another day, whatever is left will need to be safely stored:

- Uneaten and still-good meat, fish, and dips should go into plastic storage containers, covered with lids and stuck back in the fridge. A good rule of thumb is to discard any perishables that have been sitting outside for more than two hours.
- Use Ziploc bags for leftover chips and garnishes.
- Cover leftover brownies with aluminum foil.
- If any serving bowls are still mostly full, just cover them with plastic wrap and stow them in the fridge.

If you have any leftover booze, stow it in the refrigerator. Liquor, such as tequila, does not need to be refrigerated, but you might slip it into the freezer for a cold shot when you really need one.

Before you leave the kitchen, put the dirty dishes in the dishwasher or stack them neatly in the sink, remembering to run water over them. You won't want to deal with any dried-on food crusts tomorrow, when you'll actually wash the dishes.

Doing Only What's Necessary

Take a quick look around your house, beginning with the backyard and taking with you two empty trash bags and a bucket. As you encounter any empty bottles, cans, cups, plates, plastic utensils, paper napkins, or other garbage, toss it immediately. Food and garbage go in one bag, and recyclables go into another. If you find half-empty glasses, bottles, or cans, dump the contents into the bucket, and toss the containers into the recycling bag.

As you fill up bags, carry them to the garbage cans and dispose of them. You might be tempted to leave the bags in a pile by your fence, but please take a moment to dispose of them properly. Ants, roaches, and rodents love nothing more than a bag of tasty-smelling garbage, so to prevent further cleanup in the morning, take the time to trash the bags tonight. As you find the bucket filling up (gross!), empty it down the drain.

Before you leave the yard, make sure you pick up anything that might become damaged if left out overnight. Dew, air, or critters could harm some

caution You might feel that you just don't need to do this mandatory cleanup: You're tired, your feet hurt, and you want to go to bed. Tough cookies! Aside from the fact that you won't want to look at a house and yard full of trash the next morning, you really do need to dispose of anything that was eaten upon. It's neither safe nor hygienic to allow food remains to linger while you sleep. It will only take about a half hour to toss all the garbage, so buck up and get the job done. Everything else can wait until tomorrow.

of your décor, so be sure to pick up these items and stash them in the house—you can put them away tomorrow.

After the yard is clean, take a quick tour of the house, beginning with the living room and stopping in every room, including those that you hadn't planned to open to guests. Look for burning candles (blow them out!), trash, food, or anything else that doesn't belong. Toss these items into the appropriate bag or bucket, and keep moving.

tip If you find anything your guests left behind, such as purses, coats, keys, or other personal items, stow them in a bag or basket to deal with later. By placing these items in a centralized location, you'll save time and energy when guests call, looking for these items.

After you've hit every room in your house—don't forget the front porch!—toss the last of the trash and recycling, empty the bucket one last time, and pat yourself on the back. You have now done the bare minimum of cleanup, and you are free to go to bed (or polish off the last of the premium tequila).

Day-After Cleaning Up

If you have enough energy, by all means clean the entire house before you go to bed. However, most hosts will find they are exhausted after they finish the mandatory cleanup. Don't feel guilty for putting off everything else until the next day. You just gave a party for 50 people—it's time for *you* to relax!

The next day, however, you will need to buckle down and dispose of your mess. Don't worry—it's not that hard.

You'll Need

- ❏ Party closet bin
- ❏ Large empty boxes, bins, or baskets (2)
- ❏ Broom and dustpan
- ❏ Garbage bags
- ❏ Cleaning supplies

Begin by tackling your décor and any other items you bought or borrowed specifically for the party. On your table (or another large, horizontal surface), place three containers: the bin you use for your party closet, as well as two large bins for items you borrowed and items your guests left behind:

- In your party closet bin, store anything you can use for your next party, such as unused paper plates, utensils, cups, napkins, balloons, candles, or other décor.

- In one of the empty boxes or bins, place anything your guests left behind, including the items you collected last night. As you tidy your house, you're bound to find a few more things—lipsticks, cell phones, keys—under the sofa cushions. Stash these items in the lost-and-found box as you unearth them.

- In the last box, place any items you borrowed for the party. By locating these things in one box, you can later stash it in the trunk of your car for easy return.

Work through your house, room by room, collecting and sorting anything that doesn't belong and tossing any trash you missed the night before. Use your three bins, and stay on the lookout for any CDs, books, or magazines that wandered into other rooms of the house.

After you've cleared your home of any party items, take a look around the front and back yards, picking up and putting away anything you brought out for the party. Toss any garbage.

tip As you collect them, stack your CDs next to the stereo. When you're finished cleaning, put them all away. If you use jewel cases to store your CDs, take a peek inside to ensure the right CD is inside the case. Party guests seem to enjoy playing musical jewel cases.

Next, clean the kitchen. If you followed my grandmother's adage and cleaned while you cooked, your job will be easy. However, because few inexperienced cooks are able to prepare a huge meal *and* clean up after it at the same time, don't feel too bad if your kitchen looks like, well, a kitchen exploded in it. Begin with the dirty dishes, and move on to the countertops, appliances, and floors.

After you've cleared the debris away and cleaned your kitchen, sweep the floors and empty the trashcans in every room. Pay special attention to the area under the tree, where your guests bashed the piñata, which should be covered with a layer of toys and piñata entrails.

At this point, your house should be looking pretty good. Because you cleaned it before the party, you're really only removing the layer of trash that accumulated the day before. If you feel like cleaning the whole house again, have at it. Personally, I think it would be more fun to relax with a leftover margarita, but that's just me.

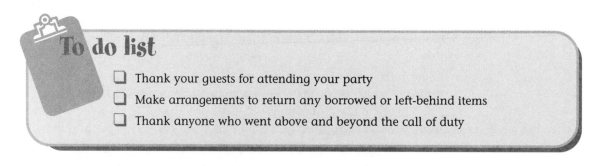

To do list

- ☐ Thank your guests for attending your party
- ☐ Make arrangements to return any borrowed or left-behind items
- ☐ Thank anyone who went above and beyond the call of duty

Thanking Your Guests

When you're finished cleaning up after your guests, it's time to thank them. Although it might seem strange to thank someone for attending a party on which you spent so much time, effort, and money, sending out a thank-you email is a nice touch that will bring your party-planning full circle. Really, is it possible to be *too* polite?

Remaining Realistic

Thanking all your guests is only realistic if you use email, especially after a party for 50 people. Compose a brief message, thanking your guests for making your party a wonderful event, and send it to everyone who attended.

As you compose your email, don't be self-congratulatory. Your guests don't need to be reminded that you hosted a fabulous party. The point of sending this email is to give your guests a warm, fuzzy feeling as they remember what a great time they had. Try to send out this email the day after your party.

> **caution** Not many people enjoy having their email address displayed for 50 other people, even if they did just spend the evening partying with them. Remember to use the BCC function on your email program, which will hide the addresses of everyone receiving the email.

Disposing of Other People's Stuff

Before you send your email message, take a look through your lost-and-found box. If you see anything that seems especially valuable, such as purses, keys, wallets, or cell phones, add a note to your thank-you message, letting your guests know you found several things that they might want back. Hopefully, you'll receive return messages claiming all the left-behind items.

Send an additional email message to anyone who loaned you something they didn't take home with them, such as the sombreros or CDs from your Mexican Fiesta, asking the best time and method for returning these items to their owners. Don't expect your guests to return for these items; courteously ask them for their preferences in getting their items back to them.

Thanking Your Helpers

Turn off your computer and get out some thank-you notes: You'll need to send a card to several kind souls, including

- Anyone who brought you a hostess gift, including bottles of wine or tequila. You do *not* need to send a note to folks who brought beer, as this "gift" was requested on the invitation.

- Anyone who performed an extraordinary act of kindness, such as going to the store for you and refusing to accept reimbursement.

- Anyone who helped you with something awkward during the party, such as those who helped babysit intoxicated guests or helped you deal with a potentially disastrous situation.

- Anyone who spent more than 15 minutes helping you with tasks you really should have completed before the guests arrived.

- Anyone who loaned you several items, especially if those items were critical to the success of your party.

Sending handwritten thank-you notes might seem old-fashioned, but it's a really nice touch. You don't need to write more than a sentence or two (ever wonder why thank-you notes are so small?), just thank your helpers for their efforts. Send out these notes within three days of your party.

Summary

Congratulations! You've just planned, shopped for, prepared for, hosted, and cleaned up after a very successful party. In the next section, "Part III, Variations on a Theme," you'll use the skills you learned in this section, "Part II, The Perfect Party," to plan and host a variety of parties, including holiday, occasion, meal, and theme parties.

Part III

Variations on a Theme

Holiday Parties

9

Now that you have mastered the art of planning a party, it's time to put those skills to use with a variety of parties celebrating annual holidays.

For each party, I'll give you a planning outline, including ideas for the date, theme, budget, venue, guest list, invitations, menu, décor, favors, music, and entertainment/activities. Although I'll outline each party to reflect a primarily midrange budget, I'll also include tips for fancifying or economizing, as well as shopping and to-do lists for each party.

As you read through these outlines, keep in mind your own party style. Whether you are classy or kitschy, modern or traditional, casual or formal, you will want to use your creativity and personal sense of style to plan the party *you* want to give.

Although I've given you suggestions, you should always feel free to alter, omit, or add ideas. Allow your personality to show throw in each party you plan—add your own unique touches to the menu, the décor, the theme, and the invitations.

You'll still need to follow the guidelines in "Part II: The Perfect Party," so take a moment to review the process for planning each party. All you'll need to do is apply that process to the outlines in this chapter, and you'll find that planning a fabulous party really is fast and simple.

New Year's Day Hangover Party

Instead of hosting yet another New Year's Eve party, why not break with tradition and throw a party on New Year's *Day*? Yes, you and your friends might feel a little worse for wear after the preceding night's festivities, but as most of you will have the day off from work, why not recuperate together? Misery loves company!

note For recipes, please refer to the online chapters in "Eating and Drinking."

You'll Need

- ❏ Ingredients for each of the recipes and any serving tools
- ❏ Decorative computer paper
- ❏ Ribbon or twine
- ❏ Incense, scented oil and burners, and a water fountain
- ❏ Aspirin, ibuprofen, Pepto-Bismol, antacid, Tums, and other post-drinking remedies, such as those recommended in the sidebar, "Hangover Remedies"
- ❏ Pillows, scarves, candles, and throw blankets
- ❏ CDs
- ❏ DVDs or videos

Date, Theme, Budget, and Venue

New Year's Day—January 1st at about 3:00 p.m.

Comfort and recuperation theme—Invite guests to wear pajamas, sweats, and slippers; encourage them to tumble out of bed, bathe if they can muster the strength, and arrive at your house in "come as you are" state.

Very low budget—About $5 per person.

Your living room or entertainment room venue—You will want your guests to be comfortable, cozy, and ensconced in pillows.

Guest List and Invitations

Your guest list should include from 6 to 20 people. If you were out late partying the night before, make sure you invite those same guests—although not all of them might be able to make it. Also invite any other close friends or friends-of-friends.

Unless you know them very well, co-workers might not be appropriate guests—don't invite anyone who might not appreciate the party or your state of mind!

Because this party is extremely casual in tone, using a web-based system is probably the easiest way to issue invitations. If you'd like, you can also send out inexpensive paper invitations at least six weeks ahead of time; the holidays are busy times, and you want to give people plenty of notice, even for a casual gathering.

> **tip** Make sure your guests understand the nature of your party! On your invitations, stress that this will be a calm, soothing, casual gathering of likewise incapacitated individuals.

Menu

Keep the menu simple, limited to comfort foods that your guests will enjoy, even if their stomachs are sour. Here's my suggested menu:

- **Finger foods**—Grandma's Chicken Wings, Classic Spinach Dip, cheese-and-cracker plate
- **Side dish**—Market Fresh Pasta Salad
- **Main dish**—Giant Hamburger Sandwich
- **Dessert**—Beer Cake
- **Beverages**—Coffee bar, selection of herbal teas, and plenty of cold water—because this party is sober in nature, ask guests to BYOB if they want alcohol.

Keep in mind that many people recover from serious partying by enjoying a meaty meal, so the Giant Hamburger Sandwich will be perfect. The pasta salad is hearty enough to serve as an entree for any vegetarian guests that might attend.

If you'd like to host a more elegant affair, switch out the main course to a catered deli platter that includes gourmet meats and cheeses; sandwich-sized bread slices; and relishes, spreads, and condiments. You'll spend more money, but you'll eliminate most of the cooking and present more glamorous fare.

Décor and Favors

Although this party is low-key, you can still have fun with the décor. Try a few of these ideas:

- **Dim lighting**—Pull the drapes or shades over the windows; dim the overhead lights; drape sheer, colored scarves over any bright lights; and light a few candles.

- **Create a soothing atmosphere**—Light incense or scented-oil burners and, if you have one, display a water fountain for the soothing sound of trickling water.

- **Create comfort**—Drape throw blankets on the couch and chairs, and pile pillows on the floor for luxurious extra seating.

- **Play up the theme**—Create a "buffet table" of over-the-counter medication, including aspirin; ibuprofen; Pepto-Bismol; antacid; Tums; and other, sillier, post-drinking remedies, such as those recommended in the sidebar, "Hangover Remedies."

caution

Don't forget about the dangers of open flames and material touching light bulbs. If you don't feel vigilant enough to mind these potential risks, eliminate them.

For your favors, re-create copies of the sidebar, "Hangover Remedies" on fun computer paper you select from your local office-supply or stationery store. Roll up each paper and tie with a bit of ribbon.

Music and Entertainment

Keep the music in tone with the theme of this party: mellow. Select soft classic rock, contemporary R&B, jazz standards, classical, instrumental, or mellow world music. Here are a few of my favorites:

- *The Book of Secrets*, Loreena McKennitt
- *Ella Fitzgerald Sings the Cole Porter Songbook*, Ella Fitzgerald
- *Essential Simon & Garfunkel*, Paul Simon and Art Garfunkel

Because the brain activity is likely to be low, DVDs/videos of silly movies are perfect entertainment for this type of party. If you'd like, you can focus the party around the viewing. You can keep the sound on "mute" if your guests are enjoying their conversations.

Although you can certainly rent a new movie, consider classic comedies:

- *Sixteen Candles*
- *Buffy the Vampire Slayer: The Movie*
- *Sex and the City: Season 1*
- *Monty Python's The Meaning of Life*
- *George Carlin: Jammin' in New York/Doin' It Again*

Also consider taping the "Rose Parade" early that morning and holding your own, private viewing, complete with commentary.

Because you will probably be celebrating the night before your party and need the morning hours to sleep in, do as much of the party planning as you can ahead of time. The party menu is especially conducive to advance preparation: You can prepare and cook everything ahead of time, except the Giant Hamburger Sandwich, which is quick to fix and cook.

HANGOVER REMEDIES

If you don't remember to begin your celebrating with a full belly and end it with plenty of water, you'll probably feel a bit nasty the next day. As you take your pharmacy-recommended, over-the-counter medication, amuse yourself with these off-the-wall hangover "cures" (just for fun, please—don't actually ingest this stuff!):

* Swallow six raw owl's eggs in quick succession.

* Get plenty of well-dried Jackalope droppings, and make them into a strong tea with hot water. Strain and drink every 30 minutes.

* Take 12 salted herrings, one cup of cider vinegar, three juniper berries, cloves and peppercorn to taste, and a dash of water. Blend together and drink slowly.

* Warm a cup of milk, and then gently add a teaspoon of fine soot from your chimney. Drink slowly. Repeat after 30 minutes.

* Drink a jigger of Pepto-Bismol laced with flat Coke from a can left over from the night before— check the can first for cigarette butts.

* Eat a hearty bowl of menudo (boiled tripe stew) first thing in the morning.

* Brew a pot of coffee with tonic water, orange juice, and honey.

* Quaff a "Red-Eye"—whiskey, coffee, Tabasco sauce, a raw egg, pepper, and orange juice, blended together.

* Stick 13 pins into the cork of the bottle that gave you the hangover.

If none of these cures are to your liking, you might try sleep, water, coffee, fried eggs and bacon, a screwdriver or Bloody Mary, and more sleep, in that order.

Valentine's Day Bitter Party

Unless you are part of a romantic twosome, Valentine's Day can be really painful, mildly irritating, or just plain boring. This year, offer your single friends a retreat from the sappy madness by hosting a bitter party, at which love is not celebrated, but exorcized.

You'll Need

- ❏ Ingredients for each of the recipes and any serving tools
- ❏ Paper invitations
- ❏ Balloons, streamers, and other décor
- ❏ Ice
- ❏ CDs
- ❏ Black netting, candy, and black ribbon
- ❏ Fireplace, shredder, or scissors

Date, Theme, Budget, and Venue

Valentine's Day—February 14th at about 8:00 p.m.

Valentine's Day painted black theme—As you plan the party, proceed as if you were planning a traditional Valentine's Day shindig, but try to find the dark side of every element, as detailed next. Allow your sense of humor to rule your planning—this event should be funny, not dismal.

Low to midrange budget—Anywhere from $5 to $15 per person.

Your home venue—This party will most resemble a cocktail party, and things might get a little crazy. Stay home, where it's safe!

Guest List and Invitations

This is a party for your single friends, only. Don't invite anyone who thinks love rules; focus on your "love bites" buddies. Invite anywhere from 10 to 30 people, mixing the guest list with men and women.

Splurge a little and buy traditional Valentine's Day invitations at a stationery or party store, and then doctor the invitations to reflect your party's theme. For example, a skull-and-crossbones drawn or stamped over a cheesy, flowery, or kid's-party invitation will be quite effective. Use your computer to create your own party details and information (time, date, and so forth), and paste this information over the preprinted info. Or, if your invitations invite it, modify the current language with a black, felt-tipped pen. Send out a month ahead of time.

Menu

Because this party is really a cocktail party in disguise, serve an assortment of appetizers, red drinks, and one theme-appropriate dessert.

- **Appetizers**—Pesto Crostini with Cherry Tomatoes, Figs in a Blanket, Prosciutto and Melon, Baked Garlic, two or three Things Shoved on a Stick, a Quickie Dip, and a tray of crackers.

> **tip** Look at dollar stores or large liquor stores for plastic skewers you can spray-paint black (be sure to use nontoxic paint). Depending on your area, you might even be able to find fancy toothpicks decorated with black cellophane!

- **Dessert**—Vanilla or chocolate cupcakes frosted with black frosting and garnished with a red-hot heart. Buy cupcake mix and vanilla icing, and use black food coloring gel or paste to turn the icing a spooky color.

- **Beverages**—Keep the red theme going by serving Cosmopolitans and Very Berry Lemonade (spiked or sober). Use skewered black gumdrops to garnish individual glasses.

Because the menu already contains a combination of upscale and budget-friendly dishes, add additional pizzazz to your event by beefing up the beverage bar. In addition to the two drinks I recommended, add a full bar to your party, and offer a selection of red-and-black garnishes, such as maraschino cherries and black olives.

To save money and still host an appetizing event, cut out the pricier appetizers—Pesto Crostini with Cherry Tomatoes and Figs in a Blanket—and replace them with an inexpensive party tray of sliced deli meats, cheeses, condiments, and crackers from Costco.

Décor and Favors

Create a Valentine's Day–turned-evil décor. Scour discount, dollar, and party stores for traditional V-Day and "Over the Hill" décor, which is usually funereal in nature: paper hearts (doctored with black pen), black-and-red streamers and balloons, and tiny cupids you can spray-paint black. Your selection will vary from store to store, so keep an open mind and think creatively.

"Don't Be Mine" sachets make great favors—many party stores offer the sweet you'll need for this favor. Look for novelty, heart-shaped candies printed with anti–Valentine's Day sentiments: "I Hate You," "Love Sucks," and "Don't Be Mine." Buy black netting and cut circles six inches in diameter. Fill with a dozen candies, and tie with black ribbon.

Music and Entertainment

I recommend loud, raucous, and unromantic music. Now is the time to pull out your high-school speed metal or punk collection! In addition to (or instead of) noisy, non-sweet tunes, look for Country-Western music or torch songs, which mourn lost or unrequited love. Look for these artists:

- Patsy Cline
- Peggy Lee
- Judy Garland
- Johnny Cash
- Marlene Dietrich

Entertain your guests with a "boyfriend bonfire." Ask your guests to bring mementos or photos of the man (or woman) who did them wrong. About three hours into the party, have a little bonfire, during which you and your guests can ceremoniously bid farewell to the losers who stole their love.

Instruct your guests to gather into a circle. One by one, each guest will destroy the memento she brought, sharing with the group one or more particularly heinous acts the ex committed, or perhaps a few choice, embarrassing flaws (hairy back, nose picker, chronic halitosis). Encourage humor, lest this intended-to-be-silly activity turn depressing.

caution   *Healthy Hostess*

BE CAREFUL! Bonfires are inherently dangerous (and might be prohibited in your area), especially when combined with drunk, depressed, and wicked-feeling guests. If you have an indoor or outdoor fireplace, proceed with caution, use common sense, and observe fire-safety rules. If you don't have a fireplace, change your activity to a "Significant Other Shredding," and use a shredder or scissors to destroy mementoes.

St. Patrick's Day Progressive Party

It always seems that every bar in town has something special going on for St. Patrick's Day. This year, instead of limiting your fun to one spot, check out several by hosting a progressive party.

You'll Need

- ❑ A car and driver
- ❑ Human décor
- ❑ Maps

Date, Theme, Budget, and Venue

St. Patrick's Day—March 17th at 6:00 p.m.

A touch o' the green theme—St. Patrick's Day is a celebration of all things Irish, including beer, corned beef, four-leaf clovers, and Celtic music. Because you and your guests will be imbibing quite a lot of beer at this progressive party, feel free to get a little silly with your planning.

Midrange budget—For progressive parties, guests pay their own way at the various establishments you visit. However, you'll want to arrange transportation for the event, for which the host should pay—unless you have very understanding friends who wouldn't mind chipping in on something fancy, such as a limo. Plan on about $20 per person.

Bars and restaurants venue—You'll need to do a bit of research when you're planning this party. Call the Irish bars and restaurants in your city of choice, and find out about their different holiday offerings. Restaurants often plan special Irish meals (corned beef!), and many bars have food, drink, and live-music specials. Talk to the bartender or manager to find out when they think the bar will be most crowded and plan your evening accordingly. You don't want to spend the whole night waiting in line to get into an overcrowded venue.

Select three to five locations, planning to hit a happy hour first (to get you lubricated), and then go somewhere for dinner. After that, visit one or two lively bars, sandwiching in at least one bar that features live music.

So you don't have to worry about drinking and driving, consider your transportation carefully. Of course, your budget will dictate your options, but you'll want to think creatively: a taxi, a rented SUV, or a minivan—or even a bus—would all work well. You'll also want to hire a driver, which will cost you about $100. Call around and find out what's available in your area, and don't forget to tip the driver at least 10% above his contracted rate.

If you have the bucks and want to make your party an event to remember, hire a limousine and driver for the entire night. You and your guests will be treated with lavish courtesy, and you won't have to worry about transportation the entire evening.

You might want to invite guests to your home or office (if appropriate) to meet up before the progression begins. A general meet-up will give folks the chance to say hello and will lend a party air to what could easily degenerate into an evening of bar hopping. You can also end the party at your place, as long as you prepare that venue accordingly.

Guest List and Invitations

Your guest list should include about 10 people. Because it can be difficult to keep track of larger amounts of people as you move from location to location, you might want to keep the guest list small. However, if you have the stamina and can afford to rent a bus, invite as many people as you would like, assuming your chosen venues can accommodate larger parties.

Because of the nature of this party, you'll probably have a lot of last-minute invitees and RSVPs. To easily keep track of your numbers, use a web-based invitation system. Don't forget to keep in mind the size of vehicle you're using and the amount of people that vehicle can safely seat.

Menu, Décor, Favors, Music, and Entertainment

The very best part of this party (from a hosting perspective) is that you are not required to provide any food or beverages. If you'd like, you can get something small, such as a cheese-and-cracker plate or St. Patrick's Day cookies, to offer at your meet-up. However, it's really not necessary.

In lieu of decorating your venue, create "human décor"—something your guests can wear that will identify them during your party. Irish-themed hats, wristbands, pins, necklaces (perhaps a day-glo green gel necklace?), or festive nametags would all suffice. Think about your guests' personalities and select something most of them will find entertaining, and then get creative and fashion something festive.

Maps make great favors for this party. After you've determined what venues you'll be hitting, create a colorful list and include a small map that shows the location of each venue (use an Internet map site to find a good map). In addition to providing your guests with something tangible by which to remember the evening (even if they remember little else), you'll ensure that no one gets lost, should he miss the bus.

You don't have to plan the music for this party. However, you might throw on a CD for your meet-up—Enya, The Pogues, or another Irish band.

To keep this event a party, and not just a bar-a-thon, plan fun activities en route to each destination. You can repurpose almost any kid's car game for your activities; here are a few to ponder:

- **Alphabet Game**—As you drive to the next venue, challenge your guests to spot objects beginning with the letters of the alphabet, beginning with "A." As adults, your selections might be very different from those of children: For example, "D" could stand for "Drunkard," and "S" for "Streetwalker." To add a theme-appropriate element to your game, instruct guests that they must limit their spotting to things related to the Emerald Isle ("Look! A drunk leprechaun!"). Because there is no "winner" for this game, it might be a good activity to get the car party started.

- **License Plate Bingo**—Challenge drivers to spell out different Irish-related words (Ireland, leprechaun, pot o'gold) with letters they spot on license plates. The first person to complete his word wins a drink on everyone else.

- **Ladder Lingo**—Begin with a St. Patrick's Day–themed word, and request the guest next to you to think of another themed word beginning with the last letter of your word. For the word "Celtic," the next word could be "Clover." Keep the game going until no one can think of another word; the loser buys the next round.

The purpose of these activities is to continue the merriment. If you find your games aren't going over well, eliminate them. Remember, as the host, it is your job to ensure your guests are happy, not annoyed or bored.

May Day Dessert Party

Traditionally observed by dancing around a maypole or anonymously gifting someone with a basket of flowers, May Day is the perfect holiday for hosting a dessert party. Because May Day is no longer celebrated with traditional elements (unless you happen to be at the Renaissance Faire), your guests won't expect over-the-top festivities; instead, you can host this simple, tasty party.

You'll Need

- ☐ Ingredients for each of the recipes and any serving tools
- ☐ Candles
- ☐ Flowers
- ☐ CDs
- ☐ Favor materials: construction paper, stapler, ribbon, basket "filling"

Date, Theme, Budget, and Venue

May 1—Schedule your party to begin at a reasonable hour, and yet after dinner. Depending upon your friends and your lifestyle, this party could begin anytime between 8:00 and 10:00 p.m.

Flowers and sweets theme—A simple party connotes a simple theme. Focus on flowers and the fare, and you'll execute this party theme without a hitch.

Low to midrange budget—Although you won't be spending money on a full menu or many other expensive elements, you can break the bank on fancy desserts. Plan to spend anywhere from $5 to $15 per person, depending upon your bank account and love of sweets.

Your living room venue—Desserts and coffee don't require much in the way of table service, so dish up your desserts at the coffee table.

tip If you and your friends enjoy galleries, museums, the theater, the opera, the ballet, or other cultural performances or events, a dessert party is a great way to end the evening. In May, many cultural organizations are ending their spring programs, so if this idea appeals to you, browse online or in your local paper to see if such an event is taking place near the date you want to host your party. Attend as a group (guests pay for their own tickets), and then reconvene at your place for the denouement.

Guest List and Invitations

Your guest list should include 8 to 20 people. This party can really accommodate any size of guest list; just be sure to invite enough people to warrant purchasing a great number of delicious desserts. Also, this party is a great way to begin or cement new friendships, so feel free to invite co-workers and neighbors, along with friends and family.

Although you could easily send paper invitations if so inclined, a web-based invitations program will do the job nicely. Make sure to explain your party on your invitations; you don't want hungry guests showing up and looking for traditional party fare.

You might also ask guests to bring their favorite dessert wine or liqueur. Conversely, you can ask guests to bring their favorite desserts—enough to serve six people—and you supply the wine. You'll receive fancier fare without the big budget.

Menu

Keep the menu simple and sweet. Plan for one and a half servings of dessert per person, which will give guests the opportunity to sample different dishes without stuffing themselves silly. (For recipes, please refer to the appropriate online chapters in "Eating and Drinking").

- **Dessert**—Cream Cheese Brownies, Mom's Strawberry Trifle; make or purchase at least three other desserts, including a variety of textures (cheesecake, fruit tart, German chocolate cake, custard, bread pudding, cookies). Dish up small portions so guests can sample several desserts.
- **Beverages**—A full coffee bar, complete with cream, sugar, cinnamon, vanilla syrup, Kahlúa, and Irish Créme. Brew regular and decaf coffee.

To fancify your dessert party, visit bakeries specializing in desserts. Purchase a wide variety of different cakes, pies, tortes, and cookies, and serve small portions on paper doilies.

To expand your selection without emptying your wallet, take the potluck approach, making one or two desserts and inviting guests to bring their favorites.

Décor and Favors

For this party to be a success, the only décor you'll need is a clean home, a few bouquets of fresh flowers, and several strategically placed candles.

Make May Day baskets for your favors. A modern take on the traditional May Day gift, these small "baskets" will delight guests at a reasonable price. Make paper cones out of construction paper (cut out an 8"-diameter circle, make a 4" cut down to the middle, roll into a cone, and staple or glue), attach a ribbon loop to the top, forming a hook. Fill the baskets with candy, cookies, fresh flowers, bundles of herbs, incense, votive candles, small toys, or anything else your sense of whimsy (or your budget) dictates.

For added flair, letter your guests' names on the baskets before you staple them together. Be sure to make a few extra for unexpected arrivals.

Music and Entertainment

Your music should be smooth and mellow. Because this party will focus on conversation, be sure to select music that won't drown out your guests' voices. Jazz, standards, new age, classical, instrumental, opera, vocals, or world music are all appropriate. Here are a few suggestions:

- *Sympatique*, Pink Martini
- *Shadow Music of Java*, Hardo Budoyo Ensemble of Wono
- *Amor e gelosia (Love and Jealousy)*, Patrizia Ciofi (Soprano), Joyce di Donato (Mezzo), Alan Curtis

No need to plan entertainment or activities for this party; the focus is on food and conversation. If you do attend an event prior to the party, stimulate conversation with a few open-ended questions about the performance or exhibit ("Wasn't the soprano lovely?").

Independence Day Block Party

Even if fireworks are illegal in your area, chances are good that at sundown, your neighbors still congregate outside, hoping to see some fire in the sky. This year, make it official with a neighborhood block party.

Because block parties are a little different than other types of parties, you'll need to approach this event as a group party, rather than one you plan yourself. Although your job as the coordinator is to keep track of the logistics—keeping a checklist of what needs to be done, inviting the neighbors, and establishing ground rules—you'll want to delegate the rest of the work in a way that ensures everyone feels included, but not overloaded.

Begin planning this party by speaking to everyone on your street and making sure they want to participate. If some of your neighbors aren't interested, don't pressure them to join—they might change their minds later on, but even if they don't, it's their decision.

Next, pick a night for a planning meeting—at least a month before the party date— and print up flyers detailing when and where (your house) the meeting will take place, as well as a short list of topics you'll cover. This meeting should only be about an hour, and you'll want to serve cookies and coffee. At the meeting, you'll want to discuss the following:

- **Party date and time**
- **Logistics**—Will you block off the street? Will you rent tables and set up the food in the middle of the street, or will each family set up a table in front of their home?
- **Food**—Will each family fix a meal to share, or will you potluck it, with each household providing a different dish?
- **Guests**—Are outside guests welcome, or would your neighbors prefer to limit the guest list to neighborhood residents only?
- **Fireworks**—If they are legal in your city, will each family provide their own assortment, and then enjoy them with the rest of the neighborhood? Or will you take donations from each household and buy a bulk assortment?
- **Cleanup**—Will everyone be responsible for cleaning up their own mess, or do you want to assign different people to each task?
- **Permits**—One person (probably you) will need to contact the appropriate city agency and determine the procedure for blocking off your street. Because the related fees usually aren't high, you can probably pay for the permit yourself; however, if the cost is prohibitive, you'll need to take up a collection from the neighbors.

After you've covered all the details and assigned tasks, trust your neighbors to carry through their assignments. Call each person a week ahead of the party to check in.

As soon as the idea for a block party begins to surface, investigate your community's particular regulations for such events. Permits can take time to process, so start early.

Keep good records of your planning! At your kickoff meeting, circulate a clipboard and ask everyone to list their household's contact person and phone number. Next to each name, record any assigned tasks. When you call to check in the week before the party, you'll have an easy time remembering who is responsible for what.

You'll Need

- ❏ Ingredients for each of the recipes and any serving tools
- ❏ Décor
- ❏ Fireworks, matches or lighter, disposal container, and piñata
- ❏ CDs and boom box
- ❏ Tables and chairs; lawn chairs and blankets

Date, Theme, Budget, and Venue

July 4th—If Independence Day falls on a weekend, you're all set. However, if it falls on a weekday, you'll need to talk to your neighbors and determine a date that works for everyone, generally the Saturday closest to the fourth of July. Begin your block party in the midafternoon, at about 3:00 p.m., which will give you plenty of time to eat, chat, and clean up before dark.

Hey, baby, it's the fourth of July! theme—On the official day of our country's birth, celebrate in style with all things American. Stores across the country will be well stocked with Independence Day merchandise, so you should have no trouble finding décor and other thematic elements.

Low to midrange budget—Each household should plan to spend a set amount of money, which you'll decide at your planning meeting. Because block parties are typically very casual, you shouldn't plan to spend more than about $50 to $75 per household. Plan to add an additional 25% onto your own budget for permits, invitations, and so forth.

The street venue—Block parties take place outside, on the street where you live. Generally, block parties run from corner to corner, involving houses on both sides of the streets. However, your neighbors might wish to extend the party for several blocks. Only you know what kind of neighborhood you have, so use your knowledge of the neighbors to guide your decision.

Traditionally, the party takes place in the middle of the street, with both ends blocked off to traffic. People can wheel their grills out to the driveway, where they'll prepare the food, and then serve the meal on tables set up in the middle of the street.

You can also take a "street fair" approach, with each family setting up a food station and table in front of their houses. Guests can wander up and down the street, stopping at different houses and sampling the fare and conversation.

Guest List and Invitations

Everyone in the neighborhood is invited, of course; at your planning meeting, you should discuss whether additional friends and family are welcome. There really is no limit to how many people can attend a block party—20 or 200—you'll want to arrive at a decision with your neighbors, and then check with the city to ensure your planned guest list doesn't exceed local restrictions.

If your neighbors are amenable, you might consider inviting additional guests: regular delivery or service people (mail carriers, water delivery people), owners and employees of local businesses, or people from nearby streets.

After you've set all the logistics, create a one-page flyer that details all your party details. Print up the flyer on red paper, and stick a copy in each mailbox on the block. Print up enough copies to give to any additional guests; if you've decided to invite friends and family, leave a dozen flyers in each mailbox.

Menu

Depending upon your approach, you'll either be providing one dish for a potluck or a full menu that will feed several dozen. That said, following are crowd-pleasing options for each course:

- **Appetizers**—Dee's Bean Dip and tortilla chips, onion dip and potato chips
- **Side dishes**—Mostly Fresh Fruit Salad, Terry Wilksen's Summer Salad
- **Main course**—Green Grocer's Pasta Primavera, grilled sausages on sandwich rolls with mustard and grilled onions
- **Dessert**—Mom's Strawberry Trifle, Cream Cheese Brownies
- **Beverages**—Sangria, Cranberry Cocktail Punch Cooler

Preparing group-sized portions can wreak havoc on your budget. If you're watching your budget, choose the Green Grocer's Pasta Primavera as your entree. You'll provide tasty fare without emptying your bank account.

If you've elected to have a potluck, select your dish from the preceding menu; if you've opted for the full-meal approach, select one item from each course.

Décor and Favors

Have fun with a red, white, and blue décor! Shop for inexpensive red, white, and blue balloons, streamers, and paper cutouts. Make sure you hang an American flag in front of your house, and purchase smaller flags to stick in plants or on the lawn.

Instead of providing individual favors for each guest, which might not be realistic if you're having a large party, set up a doggie refreshment stand in front of your house. Provide large bowls of fresh water and purchase or bake nutritious dog cookies. Package two or three cookies in plastic bags (tied with red, white, and blue ribbon!) for folks whose dogs are not in attendance.

If you have the budget and the inclination, create a more elaborate favor. Few people have read the Declaration of Independence, so provide your guests with their own, aged-looking copy. Look online for the text to the Declaration, and copy it, adjusting the font size so that it fits on one page. Print out several dozen copies, soak them in weak coffee, and allow the pages to dry thoroughly; you can also purchase antiqued paper at most office supply stores. Roll up each copy and tie with a red-white-and-blue ribbon, and offer them in a basket in front of your house.

Music and Entertainment

Fourth-of-July music should be boisterous and crowd-pleasing. Set up a boom box in front of your house and play a variety of music that will entertain the various types of people on your street. In other words, choose kid-friendly music that doesn't contain offensive lyrics. Here are a few ideas to get you started:

- *Louisiana Gumbo*, Putumayo
- *Stevie Wonder—The Definitive Collection*, Stevie Wonder
- *Other Voices, Other Rooms*, Nanci Griffith

Remember that you're sharing your space with other people, and adjust the volume accordingly. If people are rocking out on your lawn, pump up the volume; otherwise, keep it adjusted to a level that won't intrude on the party.

If your city allows fireworks, plan a stellar display to end the party. Start at dusk, pooling your neighborhood resources for enough fireworks to last about 45 minutes. Suggest that neighbors set up lawn chairs and fetch blankets if it gets chilly. Take turns lighting the fireworks, allowing each adult to set off a few, if they so desire.

If fireworks aren't allowed in your area, pick up a piñata or plan another kid-friendly finale.

Labor Day Picnic

Although you might be tempted to spend Labor Day doing anything *but* labor, a picnic is a nice way to gather with friends without breaking (much of) a sweat. Instead of planning another barbecue or beach party, head for the park, where you can relax with your friends and take in a little nature.

caution *Healthy Hostess*

Fill a bucket or trashcan about halfway with water, in which you can discard spent fireworks, matches, and anything else that has encountered fire. The next day, you can drain out the water and toss the whole soggy mess.

tip If you aren't allowed to set off fireworks, check with city hall to see if they are planning any public displays. For example, from my mother's front yard, we can view the spectacular our city council puts on each year. If you aren't as fortunate as my mom, consider ending your evening with a carpool to the nearest display. This might be too much effort for such a large party, but the idea is worth mentioning in your planning meeting. Even if only a small group wants to go, it would still be a fun ending to the evening.

You'll Need

- ❑ Ingredients for each of the recipes and any serving tools, including metal skewers for the marshmallow toasting
- ❑ Tools to clean picnic site (before and after picnic): paper towels, all-purpose cleaner, trash bags, metal dustpan for ashes, whisk broom
- ❑ Tools to prepare grill: oven cleaner (really good for getting dried-on gunk off frequently used grills), wire brush, charcoal, lighter fluid, matches or lighter
- ❑ Materials for favors: tumblers, craft/paint pens
- ❑ Lawn and/or board games
- ❑ Balloons
- ❑ Large cooler, drink cooler for punch, ice

Date, Theme, Budget, and Venue

Labor Day—Traditionally observed the first Monday in September; check your calendar for this year's date. Arrive at your picnic site at about noon, and plan to eat at about 2:00 p.m.

All play and no work theme—Labor Day is a celebration of the workers and their families, so this year, honor your hard-working guests with a day filled with leisure. Plan a simple menu; take care of all the arrangements; purchase, borrow, or rent a few lawn games; and try to enjoy yourself.

Low budget—This simple party should only run you about $8 a person, if that.

The park venue—Do a little Internet research to find a park near you that allows you to reserve picnic sites. As many other people are likely to spend the day in the park, you'll want to ensure you have a great spot. Look for a park that has roomy sites with picnic tables, grills, and trashcans, as well as a public restroom nearby. You might have to make a few calls to find the right park with all your desired amenities.

Be sure to reserve your site as far ahead of time as possible because the really good spots are sure to fill up fast. Rental permits are usually inexpensive—less than $20—and you might even be able to make the arrangements online or over the phone.

Guest List and Invitations

Your guest list should include about 20 people. Invite friends, co-workers, and family; if you want to invite children, make sure your party is appropriate for all ages. You might also find out if dogs are permitted at your park of choice and, if so, invite guests to bring their pets.

For this casual party, Internet invitations are perfect. You can keep track of your guests and what they choose to bring, which will save you time and money.

Menu

Plan a potluck menu. Although you'll provide the basics, ask each guest to bring one item to contribute to the picnic, such as condiments, garnishes, buns, chips, cookies, ice, soda, paper plates, plastic utensils, cups, side dishes, and bottled water. For your part, plan this menu:

- **Appetizers**—Deviled eggs, onion dip and potato chips, cheese and crackers
- **Side dishes**—Terry Wilksen's Summer Salad, grilled corn on the cob, watermelon
- **Main course**—Grilled sausages, hamburgers, and veggie burgers (garnishes: onion, lettuce, tomato, and cheese)
- **Dessert**—Toasted marshmallows
- **Beverages**—Cranberry Cocktail Punch Cooler (bring a bottle of vodka to spike the cooler if alcohol is permitted at your picnic site), soda, bottled water

If you have enough guests attending, ask them to bring menu items, such as cheese and crackers, onion dip and potato chips, or marshmallows. You can also ask them to supplement the menu with their own salads, desserts, or items to grill. Most web-based invitation systems enable you to keep track of what your guests are bringing, so check a few days before the party to ensure that you have the basics covered.

To add a touch of merriment to your party, spike the watermelon with vodka. A week before the party, cut a 1"-diameter hole in the watermelon and empty in the contents of a 750ml bottle of vodka (the cheap stuff is fine). Refrigerate until the day of the party.

If you have a tight budget, eliminate the hamburgers and switch the sausages to hot dogs. Your guests won't mind at all because park picnics are typically low-tech.

Décor and Favors

Instead of focusing on a particular theme, dress your picnic in simple, classic décor. Look for red-and-white checkered tablecloths at your local discount or dollar store.

Cover the picnic table, and spread a few table-cloths on the lawn area for additional seating. Add white cloth or festive paper napkins, and you don't need much else—besides the food!

After Independence Day, many stores, such as Wal-Mart or Target, offer deep discounts on their summer merchandise. Plan ahead and stock up on coolers, lawn games, grilling tools, cutlery, dishes, and picnic baskets. You'll use these items long after your Labor Day picnic, so consider them as an investment.

> **tip** Don't forget the balloons! Purchase a few helium-inflated mylars and tie them at your picnic area so that guests are able to find you easily. If the park is particularly difficult to navigate, tie mylars in a trail from the parking area to your picnic site.

Consider offering personalized tumblers as favors. As you're shopping at end-of-summer sales or dollar stores, pick up enough large (32 to 64 oz.), plastic tumblers for all your guests.

Choose unadorned tumblers in different colors and use craft or paint pens to customize each tumbler with your guests' names. Then, at the picnic, each guest will have his own cup from which to drink, eliminating a great deal of trash. After the party, guests can take the cups home with them and use them for their own picnics.

Be sure to bring extra cups and your writing materials to the picnic; it will only take moments to make favors for unexpected guests.

Music and Entertainment

Bring a boom box (and extra batteries!) and play your favorite party music. Here are a few CDs that would work well:

- *Beauty & The Beat*, Go-Go's
- *Songs You Know by Heart*, Jimmy Buffett
- *The Immaculate Collection*, Madonna

Remember that you are sharing public space, and adjust the volume accordingly.

Bring an assortment of fun games intended to be played on a lawn, such as croquet, badminton, volleyball, lawn darts, or beanbag tic-tac-toe. Check your picnic site first to see how much room you have. If you're too limited for big-area games, bring a variety of board games, such as Scrabble, Monopoly, Trivial Pursuit, or Cranium. Don't force anyone to play; just make the games available for anyone who's interested.

As you're toasting marshmallows or polishing off the last of the spiked watermelon, start a little game in which you invite people to share the thing they hate most about their jobs. Then, after everyone has had a turn, get everyone in the mood to return to work by inviting them to share the thing they love best about their jobs.

ALTERNATIVE HOLIDAY CELEBRATIONS

If you're tired of throwing parties on traditional holidays, plan a party for a seldom-celebrated special day, such as one of the following (all of which are real observances!):

* **Trivia Day (January 4)**—Games night, featuring Trivial Pursuit.

* **Random Acts of Kindness Day (February 17)**—Progressive party in which you arrange a group of friends to perform good deeds for strangers (helping an overburdened mother or disabled person at the grocery store, working at a food bank), and then enjoy a round at a local bar.

* **Earth Day (April 22)**—A tree-planting or gardening party, with a picnic as the focus.

* **Towel Day (May 25)**—A costume party in which guests make their getups from towels.

* **Best Friends Day (June 8)**—A brunch honoring best friends—yours and other people's.

* **National Hot Dog Day (July 22)**—Weiner roast! You can also invite your friends with dachshunds.

* **National Homeless Animals Day (August 20)**—A pet adoption or dog party.

* **Talk Like a Pirate Day (September 19)**—A costume party in which guests dress and talk like pirates.

* **National Coming Out Day (October 11)**—A celebration for all your gay, lesbian, bisexual, or trans-gendered friends.

* **Sandwich Day (November 3)**—A potluck to which your guests bring their favorite sandwiches to share.

* **Human Rights Day (December 10)**—A fundraising party in which guests each bring a cash contri-bution, which you donate to a human-rights organization, such as Amnesty International.

The point is that you can really throw a party for any occasion, even those you perceive as being silly. For more information on unusual holidays, search online. Believe it or not, there is a holiday for almost everything!

Halloween Costume Party

The classic party for Halloween, a costume party encourages even the most boring adults to find their inner children, dressing up in costumes that range from silly to spectacular. In this chapter, I'll discuss a traditional Halloween costume party; for variations, please refer to the "Costume Party" section in Chapter 11, "Throwing a Theme Party."

You'll Need

❏ Ingredients for each of the recipes and any serving tools you'll need

❏ Orange and black construction paper

❏ Orange or white 5"×7" envelopes

❏ Glue

❏ An assortment of Halloween stickers (spiders, cats, haunted houses, ghosts, witches, cauldrons, monsters, and so forth)—look in the scrapbooking or card-making sections of your craft store for cute, creative, or interesting flat, puffy, or three-dimensional stickers

❏ Scissors or paper cutter

❏ Glitter, paint pens, or other decorative writing instruments

❏ Black felt-tip pen

❏ Stamps

❏ Décor

❏ Favors

❏ Prizes

❏ Spooky Feel-It items

❏ Costume

❏ CDs

❏ Extra CD players/boom boxes

❏ Candy for trick-or-treaters

note Wear a costume! You can hardly expect your guests to create wonderful, creative costumes if you don't do the same. Even if you don't have a lot of time or mental energy to invest in coming up with a really clever costume, and you don't have the budget or inclination to rent one, you can still make a good showing: Purchase scrubs and go as a nurse or doctor; wear sexy (or comfy) pajamas; dress up and hang a large gift tag around your neck that reads, "To: Men" "From: God" (use "To: Women" if you happen to be male). Just do something!

Date, Theme, Budget, and Venue

Halloween—The last day of October. If the date falls on a Friday or Saturday, have the party on Halloween. Otherwise, have the party the weekend before; if you wait until the weekend following Halloween, you run the risk of losing the spooky spirit because guests become reluctant to spend one more night in this year's getups. Begin your party at 8:00 or 9:00 p.m.

Halloween! theme—All things spooky, silly, black, and orange. Pull out all the stops for this party, decorating your home to the nines, playing spooky music, offering fun activities and delicious foods, and ending the night, of course, with a costume contest. Have fun with the theme—the only thing getting between you and the most fabulous Halloween party ever thrown is your budget.

Midrange to high budget—If you have the bucks, go all out and spend up to $25 per person. Heck, spend more if Halloween is your favorite holiday and you can afford to break the bank. You don't have to go nuts with the planning; it's quite possible to have a great party on a smaller budget. However, to throw a really great Halloween party, you'll probably need to spend at least $12 a person, so plan accordingly.

Your spooky house venue—Although some Halloween aficionados turn their entire homes into haunted houses, you might not have the budget to do so. At the very least, spiff up your main party area (living room, back yard), bathroom, and entryway, and add small, thematic touches to other, less-frequented areas, such as the kitchen, office, or bedroom.

Guest List and Invitations

Your guest list should include your entire address book. Halloween is one of those great holidays that almost everyone enjoys celebrating. Share the fun with your friends, neighbors, family, and co-workers—even your nanny or dog walker! After you set your budget, invite as many people as you can swing—also be prepared for any number of extra guests because Halloween parties usually attract posses.

Paper Halloween invitations can be a lot of fun to send out. If you have the inclination, make your own! Here's an easy idea:

1. Cut construction paper into rectangles: 10"×7" black rectangles and 9"×6" orange rectangles.

2. Glue the black rectangles to the orange rectangles, centering the orange paper on the black so that a ½" margin of black paper borders the orange page.

3. Fold the card in half, with the black page on the outside. Make sure your card fits into the envelopes you'll be using. You might have to trim the edges a little.

4. Decorate the front of the card with stickers or other trim; you can also draw simple sketch outlines of Halloween figures (spiders, cats, haunted houses, ghosts, witches, cauldrons, monsters, and so forth) in glitter or paint pen (silver or gold glitter looks great).

5. On the inside of the card, use the black felt-tip pen to letter your party details: date, time, location, contact information, costume contest details, and so forth. You can also use your computer to print this information onto a white piece of paper, trim it to 4"×6", and glue it to the inside of the card.

6. Put cards into envelopes, address with black felt-tip pen, stamp, and mail.

If you don't have the time or budget to make your own Halloween party invitations, either purchase paper invitations or use an Internet-based invitation system.

Menu

Instead of spending a lot of money on a full buffet, offer a selection of scary finger foods. For each dish, create a sign on an index card and prop up next to the item. You get extra points for using a calligraphy pen or otherwise decorating the signs.

- **Appetizers**—Grandma's Chicken Wings (call them "Barbecued Bat Wings"), Dried Scabs (a mixture of dried fruit, such as cherries, cranberries, blueberries, and anything else that resembles a scab), Iptacita's Guacamole (call it "Green Ooze") served with tortilla chips, and baked garlic (label it "Vampire Bane") with sliced baguette.

- **Entree**—Make pumpkin sandwiches. Layer a slice of cheese and a slice of turkey between two pieces of bread, and use the condiment of your choice to help "glue" the whole thing together (I like a little mayo and cranberry relish). Press a pumpkin-shaped metal cookie cutter (the plastic ones don't work as well) into the sandwich and gently pull away the crust. Lift cookie cutter away and discard edges of sandwich. Arrange on a serving platter.

- **Dessert**—Pecan pumpkin pie (skip the caramel sauce and serve with a dollop of whipped topping), store-bought Halloween cookies, cream cheese brownies (cut into squares and top with raspberry sauce, which will look like blood).

- **Beverages**—Mulled Wine (serve from the stove top), Cranberry Cocktail Punch Cooler (spike with vodka, if you'd like), assorted cocktails as your budget allows.

> **tip** Don't forget the candy! If you expect trick-or-treaters, make sure you get a few (dozen?) bags of candy. Instead of waiting by the door for kids, place the bowl of candy near the door with a sign reading, "Help yourself!" Whoever is nearest the door can hold out the bowl for the kiddies.

Décor and Favors

Because entire books, magazines, and stores are devoted to Halloween décor, I won't go into great detail about creating a haunted house in your home. However, make sure you don't forget these staples:

- **Carved pumpkins**—Set these on the porch, in the foyer, in the fireplace, in the bathroom, and/or in the yards. Be sure to use candles expressly made for pumpkins, lest your gourds melt.

- **Hanging ghosts**—Blow up a balloon, cover it with a sheet, and tie the "neck" with string. Draw on a haunted face with a black marking pen.

- **Cobwebs everywhere**—Purchase by the bag at Halloween stores and hang in every room. Don't forget to stud them with spiders!

- **Dry ice**—Put small blocks in buckets with about 6" of warm water to create a foggy effect. Place buckets on the ground in various places around the room, and guests will move the fog about as they walk around. Be sure to wear heavy work gloves when handling the dry ice as it will burn bare skin.

- **Dead flowers**—Visit a floral shop a week before the party and ask for their dead blooms. Call a few weeks ahead to make these arrangements so you won't be sniped by like-minded party planners.

These basics are just a few ideas to get you started. If you want to go all out, invest in a Halloween book and do some Internet research. If you have the time, budget, and interest, you can transform your entire home into a virtual graveyard.

Because this party will be large, making individual favors will be time-consuming and expensive. Instead, visit a Halloween or dollar store and pick up a bunch of spooky toys—plastic skeletons, spider rings, chocolate-filled pirate gold, candy, and other tacky treasures—for about $.50 to $1 each. Arrange in a bowl near the bar or in the foyer, and allow guests to take whatever appeals to them.

Music and Entertainment

Halloween compilation CDs are easy to find at this time of year. Here are a few that sound great:

- *Halloween Howls*, Andrew Gold
- *Classics from the Crypt*, Various Artists
- *Halloween Hits*, Various Artists

Consider purchasing, borrowing, or renting a few Halloween or spooky sound-effect CDs, which you can play in the bathroom, "quiet" lounging room, front yard, or foyer. You'll need to borrow additional CD players or boom boxes for this effect.

I call one of my favorite Halloween party activities "Spooky Feel-It." A buffet of brains, guts, and eyeballs. What a delight for the fingertips!

You'll Need

- ❑ 10 to 15 large grapes, peeled
- ❑ ½ lb. cooked, cold spaghetti
- ❑ ½ lb. cooked, cold elbow macaroni
- ❑ Slices of American cheese, cut into irregular shapes
- ❑ Large grapefruit, peeled and halved
- ❑ 5 large cardboard boxes, at least 18" on each side
- ❑ Scissors
- ❑ Note cards
- ❑ Colored pens or pencils

Arrange the peeled grapes (eyeballs), cold spaghetti (guts), macaroni (maggots), cheese (skin), and grapefruit (brains) in separate bowls. Cut a 4"-diameter hole in the side of each box, and place a box over each bowl. Guests should be able to reach in through the holes to feel what lies beneath. Label each box as appropriate: eyeballs, guts, maggots, skin, and brains. Encourage guests to touch and squeal.

A costume contest is a natural for this party. Reward your guests for taking the trouble to attend in costume by inviting them to parade in front of the whole party. Award prizes for the three best costumes. If you can't decide who wins, let the crowd decide with rounds of applause.

If you're on a small budget and you still want to give a first-rate Halloween party, splurge on the decorations (which are relatively inexpensive), scale down on the food, and make the party BYOB, investing only in soda, water, and a small keg of beer. Make sure your invites read "BYOB," and your guests will bring enough hooch to go around. By creating great atmosphere, your guests will feel as though they are in a much fancier party than the one your small budget allowed.

note Give good prizes! Spend about $5 to $10 on the second and third prizes, and fork over $15 for the top prize. CDs, DVDs, books, movie passes, candy, nuts, and anything else that you wouldn't mind personally receiving will do nicely. Keep the prizes unisex, and wrap them in Halloween paper.

Multicultural Winter Party

As our culture becomes increasingly diverse, it's no longer appropriate to assume "the winter holidays" means Christmas. Instead of trying to decide which holiday to observe at your December party, celebrate all of them! Christmas, Hanukah, Kwanza, and Winter Solstice are all lovely reasons to have a party; with a multicultural winter party, you can honor all your guests and their spiritual beliefs.

You'll Need

- ❑ Ingredients for each of the recipes and any serving tools you'll need
- ❑ Décor
- ❑ CDs
- ❑ Gifts

Date, Theme, Budget, and Venue

Saturday in December—Realistically, Christmas is the most-observed holiday in December, so you might be tempted to schedule your party close to December 25th. However, you'll be better off hosting your party earlier in the month: As December quickly fills up with parties, especially later in the month, by having your party early, you'll ensure high attendance. Begin your party at 7:00 p.m., serving dinner at 8:00.

Holiday theme—Try to split your theme evenly between all four winter holidays, mixing décor, favors, and other thematic elements to reflect Christmas, Hanukah, Kwanza, and Winter Solstice. For Christmas, use red and green colors; for Hanukah, use blue, white, and yellow; for Kwanza, use red, black, and green; for Winter Solstice, use green and brown. How you incorporate these different colors and themes is up to you: You might want to devote a corner of your house to each of the four holidays or mix them up throughout your home. For more ideas, read on to the "Décor and Favors" section.

Midrange to high budget—This is another party that can either break the bank or have a reasonable cost. If you enjoy celebrating the winter holidays and can afford a lavish party, you'll find plenty of décor, food, beverages, and favors on which to spend a bundle. However, if you don't have a ton of money to blow, then you can still have a great party by creating a wonderful, inviting atmosphere and serving delicious food. However, you won't be able to throw this party on less than $10 per person.

If you really want to have a holiday party, but have almost nothing in the bank, switch gears completely. Invite close friends to a potluck dinner or inexpensive restaurant that seats large parties (make sure your friends know that this is a Dutch-treat event, and that you are merely acting as coordinator), and have a gift exchange. You'll still celebrate the holidays with cherished friends, which is really the most important thing about holiday parties.

Your home venue—Make sure your entire home and grounds are clean, uncluttered, and organized before you begin decorating. If, like many people, you enjoy looking at holiday décor throughout the month of December, you'll want to do all the prep work on your property at the end of November, and then put up the initial holiday décor on December 1st. You can always add party décor as you get closer to your event.

Guest List and Invitations

Plan on inviting between 15 to 50 people. Holiday parties tend to be on the large side, so feel free to invite as many people as your budget allows.

If you would like to make or purchase multicultural party invitations, your guests will certainly appreciate the extra touch. However, because so many parties take place in December, you might have better luck keeping track of RSVPs if you use an Internet-based invitations program. Another benefit to using this type of system is that you can customize your electronic invitations to reflect your multicultural theme.

Menu

Depending upon the size of your guest list, you can serve this savory dinner seated or as a buffet. The Sauerbraten recipe will serve more people if you include additional side dishes, such as Garlic Mashed Potatoes, Fresh Vegetable Mix-Up, Garlicky Spinach, or Cauliflower "Mashed Potatoes."

- **Appetizers**—Stuffed Mushrooms, Pesto Crostini with Cherry Tomatoes, Figs in a Blanket, assorted things on sticks
- **Side dishes**—Sweet & Sour Cabbage, Brown-Buttered Butternut Squash, Garlkicky Spinach
- **Main course**—Grandma's Sauerbraten with Dumplings
- **Dessert**—Frosted holiday sugar cookies (look for a variety of cookie cutters that symbolize different religious holidays: stars, candles, trees, stockings) and fudge

If you're pressed for time, purchase decorated sugar cookies. Look for stars and candles, which are neutral for all spiritual beliefs, or talk to your local bakery and see if they will custom-bake a large batch of cookies to your specifications.

- **Beverages**—Eggnog, Irish coffee, mulled wine, coffee, water, and assorted sodas

If so inclined, you can add another entree to the buffet, such as a roasted turkey or goose. If you opt for fowl, remember to add stuffing to your menu—the rest of the side dishes will suffice.

Décor and Favors

Because so many resources are available for December decorating—web, books, and magazines—I won't attempt pointers in this brief section. However, I will offer a few culturally specific icons upon which you might want to focus:

- **Christmas**—Santa Claus, nativity scenes, Christmas trees, stockings, stars, bells, candles, snowflakes, reindeer, mistletoe, Yule log, snowmen, and gifts; the colors red and green.

- **Hanukah**—The menorah (candle holder with eight regular tapers and one long one), gold coins (or chocolate-filled gold coins), dreidels, and gifts; the colors blue, white, and gold.

- **Kwanza**—*Mkeka* (straw placemat), *Mazao* (fruits and vegetables), *Vibunzi/Muhindi* (ears of corn), *Kikombe cha umoja* (communal unity cup), *Kinara* and *Mishumaa saba* (candle holder with seven candles, one black, three red, and three green), and *Zawadi* (gifts that are enriching); the colors red, black, and green.

- **Winter Solstice**—Yule log; boughs of laurel, evergreen, and holly; good-luck gifts of fruit, cakes, candles, dolls, jewelry, and incense; mistletoe; and colored lights; the colors green, brown, and white.

If you enjoy having a Christmas tree, consider adding ornaments that reflect each holiday tradition.

The best holiday parties are those at which the hostess has a gift for every guest, even the unexpected. For your close friends, purchase gifts as you normally would. For more casual friends, significant others, co-workers, or neighbors, pick up inexpensive ($5 to $15) gifts you wouldn't mind receiving yourself, such as bath products, coffee, coffee cups, fruit, nuts, candy, CDs, DVDs, books, candles, incense, photo frames or small albums, kitchen gadgets, socks, slippers, note paper, cards, journals, or food items. Select gender-neutral gifts and eschew holiday-themed gifts, as you don't want to guess at your guests' religious beliefs. Also, remember to pick up and wrap about five extra gifts for unexpected guests.

tip To save a great deal of time and money, shop for your holiday gifts all year around. As you browse in discount stores, keep your eyes out for inexpensive, gender-neutral, quality gifts, such as those listed previously. In addition to keeping a well-stocked gift closet, you'll have quite a few gifts amassed by December.

Music and Entertainment

Choose multicultural holiday music. Although Christmas CDs are everywhere, you might have a more difficult time finding party music to represent Hanukah, Kwanza, and Winter Solstice. Here are a few ideas:

- *A Winter's Night*, Ensemble Galilei
- *Happy Hanukah*, Judy Rubenstein
- *Africa*, Putumayo
- *A Jazz Celebration of Christmas, Chanukah & Kwanza*, Lynette Washington, Long, Long Ago

Try to alternate CDs to play an assortment of songs from different albums; if you have a random-play feature on your CD player, use it. If your guests begin to tire of holiday music, throw on some classical, jazz, modern rock, bluegrass, or dance music.

If you are gathering together people who know one another well enough to give each other gifts (possibly several different groups of people), let your guests know you'll be hosting a gift exchange. People might wonder if they're supposed to bring gifts for everyone or if you are planning a "Secret Santa" exchange, so explain on your invitations that although you'll be giving out gifts to everyone, your guests only need bring gifts for those people to whom they'd normally give holiday gifts, if they choose. A few hours into the party, turn down the music and gather for your exchange.

If you don't want to make an activity of the gift giving, simply give guests their gifts throughout the party, spending a few minutes with each guest or group of people.

Summary

Now that you've learned how to apply the information in the first sections of this book to real-life party planning, we'll look at the different occasions for which you can host a fabulous party, including birthdays, showers, life milestones, and office parties.

Occasion Parties

10

Some occasions demand parties: birthdays, anniversaries, weddings, and new additions. Although these types of parties have traditional components, especially showers, there's no reason you can't play around with tradition and put your personal stamp on the parties you host.

For each party, I'll give you a planning outline, including ideas for the date, theme, budget, venue, guest list, invitations, menu, décor, favors, music, and entertainment/activities. Although I'll outline each party to reflect a midrange budget, I'll also include ideas about how to fancify or economize. You'll also see shopping and to-do lists for each party, which will help you get started on your planning.

As you read through these outlines, keep in mind your own party style. Whether you are classy or kitschy, modern or traditional, casual or formal, you will want to use your creativity and personal sense of style to plan the party *you* want to give.

Birthday Parties

Perhaps the most frequently given type of occasion party, birthday parties usually follow a familiar pattern: Gather, eat, open presents, have cake, leave. Although this pattern is unlikely to change (why fix what isn't broken?), you can certainly liven up familiar traditions by adding your own creative touches to the venue, décor, menu, and activities.

> **note** For recipes, please refer to the online chapters in Part V, "Eating and Drinking," at www.quepublishing.com.

You'll Need

- ❑ Ingredients for each of the recipes, as well as tools for preparing and serving menu items
- ❑ Picnic blankets (if you don't have picnic blankets, oversized beach towels, reed mats, or regular blankets will also work)
- ❑ Picnic baskets
- ❑ Ice chests/coolers for cold items
- ❑ Birthday candles and lighter or matches
- ❑ Balloons or homemade signs
- ❑ Picnic game: croquet, badminton, or Scrabble
- ❑ Music CDs
- ❑ Three wrapped prizes

Birthday Picnic

Although dinner parties, group gatherings at a restaurant, and cocktail parties are quite nice, celebrate with something a little different this year: a birthday picnic. Gather together the birthday girl's closest friends and spend the afternoon lounging in the shade, noshing on delicious food, and relaxing.

Date, Theme, Budget, and Venue

The guest of honor's birthday—If you can't have the party on your guest's actual birthday, ask her which date would be best for her. You'll likely throw the party on the weekend just before or after her special day—a Sunday afternoon would be nice for this picnic.

Simply classy theme—This picnic is a great occasion to bust out the fancy picnic basket your mom gave you last summer. Straw hats, red-and-white-checked picnic blankets, perhaps a game of croquet in the afternoon...enjoy a lazy afternoon of simple pastimes.

Midrange budget—Plan to spend about $11 or $12 per person for this picnic.

A grassy knoll venue—Depending upon your area's topography, you might host this picnic at a park, the beach, near the lake, in the woods, or even in your own backyard. All you really need is a flat, comfortable area, shade, and access to bathrooms.

Guest List and Invitations

Invite about 15 to 20 people to this party, basing your guest list on the birthday girl's preferences. Ask her who she'd like to attend—friends, family, neighbors, co-workers—and get everyone's phone number and email address. If you have a friend or two whose company you think the birthday girl might enjoy, it's entirely appropriate to invite additional guests.

If you'd like to spring for paper invitations, look for simple cards that suit your theme; you might also look for decorative computer paper at an office supply store and make your own invites.

However, using a web-based application to manage the guest list for this picnic would probably be the easiest, most efficient way to go. You can even customize your electronic invite by uploading an image of the guest of honor.

Menu

Each of these dishes is simple to make and travels well. You can make everything the night before the party, except for the green salad, which you should toss together just before serving (bring the prepared lettuce with the additional ingredients in plastic baggies or small Tupperware containers).

- **Appetizers**—Herb-Marinated Cheese with baguette slices, chilled artichokes (cook and chill the night before and serve with Cindylicious Aioli)
- **Side dishes**—Erica's Favorite Salad, Morning Melon Balls, Mediterranean Pasta
- **Main course**—Gastrointerestinal Disaster
- **Dessert**—Cookies (Stop by a bakery for an assortment of cookies, and purchase a cupcake to serve as the birthday cake. Don't forget the birthday candle!)
- **Beverages**—Limoncello

Your vegetarian friends will also enjoy this meal; Mediterranean Pasta makes for a hearty main course.

Décor and Favors

Keep the décor simple: Just the picnic blankets will do; nature will provide the rest of the party decorations. Do remember to guide guests from the parking lot to the picnic site with balloons or homemade signs. If the guest of honor appreciates extravagant touches, consider adding a few streamers and balloons to the picnic site.

Instead of favors, give out prizes for the croquet champions (or whichever game you elect to play). Purchase and wrap inexpensive, gender-neutral gifts (movie tickets, gift cards, candy), and award first, second, and third-place winners.

Music and Entertainment

Bring a boom box and an assortment of CDs the guest of honor would enjoy. If you aren't sure of your friend's tastes, opt for tunes that will set a pleasant, mellow atmosphere, such as these:

- *Graceland,* Paul Simon
- *Revival,* Gillian Welsh
- *Tracy Chapman,* Tracy Chapman

tip   Plan ahead for a day of outdoor recreation by bringing along a few necessities: sunblock, premoistened towelettes, Benadryl, matches, a first-aid kit, trash bags, insect repellant, and plenty of bottled water.

For entertainment, the birthday guest will have presents to open and a candle to blow out. Either before or after this merriment, host a picnic-appropriate game of some sort, such as croquet, badminton, or even Scrabble. If your guests are not inclined to play, simply give out the prizes arbitrarily—best lip-sync to "Fast Car," longest nap, or the best grass-blade whistler.

Celebrating Different Birthdays

You can easily adapt the picnic idea to almost any birthday celebration, even those for children or the elderly. Of course, you'll want to keep your guests in mind when you choose your picnic site. For example, children will prefer a park with a good playground, and seniors will appreciate picnic tables. Beyond choosing the venue, here are a few more ideas about how to make a birthday celebration special.

Kid Parties

Whether you're celebrating a child's birthday or simply inviting children to your party, you'll need to make special accommodations for the wee ones. Allocate more budget to favors and décor, purchasing kid-friendly decorations and small toys for each child attending. When you select your picnic games, opt for a few games that kids can play, too, such as beanbag tic-tac-toe, Twister, or the ubiquitous Candy Land. Most of the planned menu is kid-friendly, but you'll want to serve something besides Limoncello—pink lemonade, perhaps?

Milestone Birthday Parties

If your guest of honor is celebrating a particularly noteworthy date, such as his 16th, 21st, 30th, 40th, or 60th birthday, you'll want to up the celebration factor and make a slightly bigger to-do of the day. If you'd like, purchase age-appropriate décor; at the bakery, order a cake that reflects the occasion: "Sweet sixteen," "21 and Legal," or "You're All Grown Up." Please, leave the "Over the Hill" themes for someone else; few people enjoy being reminded that they will soon be eligible for a senior-citizen discount.

Surprise Parties

A surprise picnic? Why not! Enlist the help of the birthday boy's significant other—perhaps she could take her fellow to the park for a nice walk before an early dinner?—and select a picnic spot that is behind a clump of trees, over a small hill, or otherwise hidden from immediate view. A note about surprise parties: Not as many people like surprises as television would have us believe. Try to get a feel for your friend's preferences, and if you truly believe he would loathe a surprise party, please, don't give him one.

Showers

The purpose of this type of party is not only to shower the guest of honor with gifts, but to welcome her to this new phase of her life. We'll look at planning a wedding shower, but with a few minor alterations, this party can easily celebrate the birth or adoption of a child or pet.

You'll Need

- ❏ Ingredients for each of the recipes and the tools necessary for serving them
- ❏ Décor, including fresh flowers
- ❏ Items for making favors: sheer fabric or netting; dried lavender; sewing notions or craft glue; pinking or craft shears; and ribbon, lace, or other trim
- ❏ Items and prizes for shower games
- ❏ Music CDs

Wedding Shower

Usually hosted by the maid of honor or other close friend of the bride, the wedding shower was traditionally an event at which the bride was given items for her trousseau. However, wedding showers now serve more as prewedding get-togethers, a chance for the bride (and groom, if you're planning a co-ed shower) to spend a few intimate moments with guests before the big day.

If you are the maid of honor, but are operating on a very small budget, talk to the bride about asking one or two other members of the wedding party to co-host the party with you. Try to select a co-host you already know, and have a logistics meeting before you begin any planning, just to make sure you and your co-host(s) are in agreement about the division of costs and labor.

Date, Theme, Budget, and Venue

Approximately four to six weeks before the wedding—Work with the bride and groom to select a date that works for them, their family, and the rest of the wedding party. Sunday afternoons are usually the best time for wedding showers; begin at about 2:00 p.m.

Wedding theme—Talk to the bride about how you might be able to incorporate her colors or other wedding elements into the shower. Try to avoid themed showers; although they are cute, they require extensive planning and are often not worth the effort.

Low to midrange budget—You'll probably need to spend between $8 and $12 per person.

Your home or another group venue—Most showers are hosted at the home of one of the bridesmaids. However, you can also host a wedding shower in a rented space or a park. Talk to the bride about her preferences, and concede to her wishes. The one place you should *not* have the shower is at the bride's home.

Guest List and Invitations

Work with the bride and/or groom to determine the guest list. You'll probably host about 25 to 30 people, including the wedding party, friends, and other family members. If the bride wishes, a co-ed shower is perfectly acceptable.

Paper invitations are a must for a wedding shower. Try to keep the wedding colors and theme in mind when selecting the invitations, and avoid anything too cutesy.

Menu

This vegetarian menu is so hearty and filling that your guests might not even notice there's no meat!

- **Appetizers**—Stuffed Mushrooms, Classic Spinach Dip, assorted cheeses and crackers
- **Side dishes**—Spinaki, Cauliflower "Mashed Potatoes," Erica's Favorite Salad
- **Main course**—Stuffed Eggplant (cut each cooked half into halves, or use Japanese eggplants)
- **Dessert**—Low-Carb Cheesecake
- **Beverages**—Very Berry Lemonade

tip In recent years, there has been some controversy about the best way to notify guests about where the bride and groom are registered. Traditionally, no mention is to be made of gifts; if asked, the bridal party or parents of the bride and groom may divulge where the gift registry is located. However, this tradition is silly. Everyone registers, and most people use an online service (www.theknot.com or www.theweddingchannel.com) to coordinate wedding details, including the gift registry. Why make a secret of the registry, requiring guests to hunt down the gift list? Instead, include on the invitations a short note that directs guests to the registry—either the online service that contains all the information, or the two to three stores at which the bride and groom registered.

If you think that meat will really be missed, add Mom's Famous Tri-Tip Roast with Gravy and make only enough Stuffed Eggplant for half the guests.

If your budget allows, order a sheet cake from a bakery that specializes in transferring photographs to cake decorations. Use the couple's engagement photo as a template, and have the bakery reproduce the picture on a great-tasting sheet cake.

Décor and Favors

Although you'll find abundant wedding shower decorations at party stores, much of it is on the tacky side. Décor should be simple and elegant: Forgo excessive frill and focus on a few pieces of quality décor, such as the cake trimmings, the buffet setup, the flowers, and, perhaps, a special hat or corsage for the guest of honor.

For favors, arrange homemade lavender sachets in a clear glass bowl near the drinks. Even if you're a terrible sewer, lavender sachets are fast and easy to make. Purchase the following materials:

- Sheer fabric or netting; two 4" squares per guest
- Dried lavender (look online or at craft stores)
- Sewing notions (sewing machine or needles, coordinating thread) or craft glue
- Pinking or craft shears (scissors that cut a decorative pattern—look in the scrapbooking section of your craft store)
- Ribbon, lace, or other trim

Cut the two squares of fabric or netting into heart-shaped pieces (first create a paper pattern so your hearts are the right shape). Stitch or glue the edges together, leaving a 1" margin outside the stitching and a 2" gap in the stitching for stuffing. Fill the pouch loosely with lavender, and close the seam. Trim edges of heart with pinking or craft shears, leaving about ¾" of decorated material outside the stitching.

If you'd like, use ribbon, lace, or other trim to decorate each sachet. Don't go overboard—keep it simple and elegant. You might also use craft pens or paint to letter the couple's initials on the sachet, or look for monogrammed buttons or trim to add.

Music and Entertainment

Music at wedding showers should be pleasant and unobtrusive. Look for classical discs, especially wedding compilations:

- *A Day to Remember—Instrumental Music for Your Wedding Day*, The O'Neill Brothers
- *Heart Beats: Now & Forever—Timeless Wedding Songs*, Various Artists
- *Modern Bride Presents the Wedding Album*, Various Artists

As for the entertainment…in addition to opening presents, you'll feature one other activity: the shower games (see sidebar).

SHOWER GAMES

Shower games spark much controversy: Most people claim to loathe them, but game-free showers are just plain boring. My solution is to offer just two games, one of which requires no effort.

* **The Safety Pin Game**—Each guest receives a safety pin as she arrives, pinning it on her top or skirt hem (somewhere visible). Throughout the shower, guests are instructed not to cross their legs. If one guest catches another guest crossing her legs, the offending guest must surrender her safety pin to the guest who spied her. The game ends when one person has all the pins, or when the presents are opened. The person with the most pins wins.

* **The Memory Game**—A game and gift all in one, the memory game is my favorite shower activity. The host purchases a number of kitchen gadgets for the bride (measuring spoons, spatulas, wooden spoons, and so forth), about 25 items. Just after the eating winds down and prior to the bride opening the presents, bring out a tray filled with the different items. Show each gadget to the guests, briefly explaining what it's for, and then return it to the tray. After you've displayed all the items, hide the tray and give the guests three minutes to write down as many items as they can remember. The person who correctly guesses the most items wins the prize. The bride gets to keep all the gadgets, your shower gift to her.

Other Types of Showers

Weddings are not the only occasion that warrants showering a couple with gifts. Follow the same outline for a baby shower, making only a few minor alterations, and you'll be well equipped for any kind of shower.

Baby Shower

All you'll really need to change for a baby shower is the motif: switch hearts and flowers for rattles and pacifiers. You can serve the same menu, offer the same favors, and plan the same activities (for the memory game, swap baby stuff for kitchen gadgets). Keep the music mellow and select infant-themed invitations, and the mother-to-be will have a lovely afternoon.

New Pet Shower

With fewer people having babies and more people treating their pets like children, a pet shower seems perfectly appropriate, especially if the guest of honor is a dog, one of the most expensive pets. Like the baby shower, you can adapt the wedding shower outline for a pet shower, using appropriate animal-themed décor and invitations.

Singleton Shower

Like Carrie Bradshaw on HBO's *Sex and the City*, you, too, can have a Singleton Shower. Just because you aren't getting married, it doesn't mean you have to forgo matching dishes or linen. Register at a housewares store and send out the invites. If you offer a fabulous party, your guests *will* show up, gifts in hand.

Housewarming Parties

One of the few parties you throw for your own benefit, housewarming parties give you an opportunity to show off your new home to your friends and family and meet your new neighbors.

You'll Need

- ❏ Ingredients for each of the recipes and any serving tools
- ❏ Fresh flowers
- ❏ Theme-related décor
- ❏ Customized matchbooks for favors
- ❏ Music CDs
- ❏ A clean, organized home

Date, Theme, Budget, and Venue

Sunday, late afternoon, about six or eight weeks after you move in— Don't have the party until you've unpacked all the boxes and are ready to entertain. Begin the party at 4:00 p.m., and plan for it to run about four hours.

Seasonal theme—Focus your party around the season: For summer, host a beach-themed party or barbecue; in autumn, play up fall colors and the harvest; in winter, connect your housewarming with a Super Bowl party; and for spring, make fresh flowers and new life your theme.

Midrange budget—because you'll be opening your home for the first time to friends, family, and neighbors, provide a bountiful spread and elegant décor. Plan to spend about $11 to $13 per person.

Your home venue—Your new abode is the featured guest at this party, so make sure it's clean, organized, and ready to be the center of attention. You don't have to be completely finished with the decorating when you have your party—your guests will understand that you've just moved in—but you should be finished unpacking and have set up what furnishings you already have.

Guest List and Invitations

Invite about 25 to 30 people, including friends, family, co-workers, and neighbors—anyone you'd like to welcome into your home. If you don't yet know your neighbors, this is an excellent opportunity to meet them. If you live in a neighborhood that doesn't invite this sort of casual intimacy, stop by and have a chat with your neighbors before inviting them. You'll be able to determine in just a few minutes whether it would be appropriate to invite them.

Use Internet-based invitations for your housewarming party. If you plan to invite neighbors, simply print out a copy of the invitation, write a personal note at the top ("We'd love to meet you and your family!"), and leave it in their mailbox or wedged in their doorjamb.

Menu

Serve an elegant, yet hearty, buffet, a mixture of grilled and kitchen-prepared food. The Shashlik recipe stretches to fill quite a few bellies, and an assortment of delectable appetizers and side dishes round out the menu.

- **Appetizers**—Baked Garlic, Pesto Crostini with Cherry Tomatoes, Stuffed Mushrooms
- **Side dishes**—Caesar Salad to Go-Go, Spinaki, KKL's Grilled Asparagus, Zucchini-Walnut Bread
- **Main course**—Shashlik the Molokan Way
- **Dessert**—Cream Cheese Brownies, Fudge
- **Beverages**—Sangria, assorted soda, water, coffee

Because this meal is heavy on the meat-free side dishes, any vegetarian guests will have a good selection of food.

If you're on a tight budget, have an open house, instead of a housewarming party. You can eliminate the barbecue and instead serve a deli tray, a honey-baked ham, or a large assortment of finger foods. As guests come and go, they can pick a few things on which to nosh, but they won't be expecting a hearty main course.

Décor and Favors

Keep the décor simple and focused on your seasonal theme; your clean and organized home should serve as the perfect décor for this party, with seasonal floral arrangements—and, perhaps, a few bowls of fresh fruit—adding a finishing touch.

To add elegance to your party, set a lavish arrangement of flowers in each room, including the bathroom and kitchen. It's a small touch, but one that will add subtle grace to your gathering.

For favors, think "practical." I like the idea of ordering customized matchbooks containing your name, new address, and phone number. Guests will have your contact information at hand whenever they light a match.

Music and Entertainment

Select cheerful, upbeat music as the background for this party. The tunes shouldn't drown out conversation, but be loud enough to ease early arrivals into the party when the room is still relatively empty. Here are a few CDs to get you started:

- *The Look of Love*, Diana Krall
- *It Had to Be You…The Great American Songbook*, Rod Stewart
- *Motown*, Michael McDonald

You really don't need to have any entertainment at this party; conversation, food, and drink are activity enough. You might be tempted to make an event out of opening your housewarming gifts, but please resist. Although gift-giving at housewarming parties is traditionally appropriate, not everyone will bring a gift. To avoid making your empty-handed guests feel uncomfortable, unwrap any gifts as you receive them, or set them aside to open after the guests have left. Please remember to send a handwritten thank-you note for any gifts you receive.

> **tip** If you need quite a few things for your new home, consider registering at a home and bath store. Registration is usually free, so there's no harm in selecting a few items; you can also create a wish list at an online store you frequent. Many guests will ask what you need for your new home—if asked, you can direct guests to your registry.

Office Parties

Although your co-workers might not be your first choice for party guests, if you approach an office party with the same attitude as you would a party in your home, it can actually be an enjoyable event. Don't spend time or money on expensive food or décor; instead, focus on what is important: relaxing with your co-workers and, perhaps, becoming better acquainted as you honor a company or personal milestone.

You'll Need

❑ Your manager or human resources department's authorization to spend company funds

❑ Company SWAG (Stuff We All Get) for favors

Date, Theme, Budget, and Venue

Late afternoon or early evening—The actual date of your party will vary according to the event; however, it's a good idea to begin office parties in the late afternoon or even the early evening, giving co-workers a chance to clear off their desks. Because an office party toes the line between duty and pleasure, the timing of the party should do the same.

Various themes—Office parties tend to bring out the goofiness in people, so feel free to ham it up when you're planning your office-party theme, whether you're hosting a retirement, shower, bon voyage, or birthday party.

Sliding budget—Your office petty-cash fund should be paying for this party, so you'll have to talk to your manager or human resources department to determine your budget. It's probably safe to assume that your budget will be minimal, unless you are celebrating a company milestone, such as 10 years in business, the closing of a big deal, or the launch of a successful product.

Break room, conference room, or roof venue—Select a large, open space for your party, somewhere you and your co-workers can unwind and feel comfortable. If you have the budget for it, rent a private room in a restaurant or bar. You might also rent a room in a moderately priced business hotel, assuming there is one nearby.

Guest List and Invitations

Invite everyone from the departments involved; don't omit a single employee, even if he's the weird guy who sits by the copy machine. Discuss the guest list with your manager to determine whether you should invite vendors, suppliers, or other people who don't actually work for your company.

Use an Internet-based invitation system to invite guests and track RSVPs. You might also post something in the break room or other area frequented by employees.

Menu

The free food is probably the most compelling reason people attend office parties, so make sure you put your full effort into planning a great menu. Here are a few ideas for different budget ranges:

- **Low (<$10/person)**—If you don't have much to spend, focus on one menu element, such as a fabulous cake or superb finger foods. Don't try to provide booze on a low budget; instead, provide sodas and water, and do a little research so you can suggest a great venue for an "impromptu" after-party, should anyone want to grab a few drinks.

- **Midrange ($10–$20/person)**—With a little more money to spend, try to find unexpected and delicious food. If your company relies on pizza, sandwiches, or the ubiquitous "big cookie" for its regular party fare, steer clear. Consider an ethnic specialty, such as Chinese, Thai, or Indian catering; you'll find prices are lower than you think for ample amounts of quality food.

- **High (>$20/person)**—If you have a large budget, use it. Either rent a room in a great restaurant or hire a professional caterer. If you're planning to spend a fair amount of money, food-service professionals should comp you a full meal at their establishment, allowing you to enjoy the atmosphere and flavors and make an informed decision about where to host your event.

Surprise is the key to planning a successful menu for your co-workers. If you're able to brainstorm several reasonable options, go with the one that's least familiar to the people with whom you work. They'll get a kick out of trying something new, especially if it's on the company's dime.

Décor and Favors

Unless you're celebrating a birthday or other specific occasion, the décor should be minimal. If you're hosting a seated dinner, provide centerpieces; otherwise, spend your money on food, not decorations.

Favors, however, are often welcome at company parties. If your budget allows for company SWAG, provide something fun for your guests. Skip the tired t-shirt or coffee mug, and opt for something useful: a baseball cap, sweatshirt, tote bag, or thermal coffee carafe, emblazoned with a discreet company logo.

Even if you don't have the budget to spend on favors, try to provide a little something for your co-workers. Raffles are fun—spend your small budget on a few choice prizes or see whether any of your vendors can donate something. Restaurant, spa, and bookstore gift certificates make great prizes, as do more tangible prizes, such as boom boxes, CDs, books, DVDs, and other items designed to please a variety of people. If you have absolutely nothing to spend, talk to your manager or HR department about raffling off a two-hour lunch or afternoon off work.

Music and Entertainment

If your budget allows it, hire a band for your party. Stick with safe genres of music—jazz, classical, standards, pop covers, bluegrass, or light rock. Check at local universities, colleges, and music schools for inexpensive entertainment. If you can't afford a band, consider hiring a D.J., a different version of live music that will be much lighter on your budget. A good D.J. will be able to weave together different albums to produce quality dance or ambient music. If your music budget is nil, at least play a few CDs to get the party going. Ask co-workers for their recommendations and opt for albums that will appeal to nearly everyone.

If you have a large budget and want to offer entertainment, think outside the box. Although a palmist, sketch artist, hypnotist, or professional clown might seem a stale idea for a party, not many people will associate that type of professional entertainment with an office party. Casting an old favorite in a new light will lend a fun, frisky quality to your selected entertainment, giving your co-workers an easy giggle or two.

Office-Party Options

In addition to annual or milestone parties, you might find yourself called upon to host a few smaller parties for co-workers, especially if you have an administrative or human resources position.

> **caution** Do not get drunk at your company party. Drinking too much can loosen your tongue, your libido, or your common sense, leading you to perform acts you would otherwise find embarrassing, such as Xeroxing your butt, making a pass at a co-worker, or telling off your boss. Be sensible and drink only in moderation (or not at all). You can celebrate your successful party later, in the safety and privacy of your own home.

Retirement and Bon Voyage Parties

If someone retires after decades of service, a banquet or other large celebration is customary. However, these days it is more likely that a co-worker is switching jobs, departments, or companies, so a bon voyage might be a more frequent request. Keep the festivities limited to those in the guest of honor's department, and include any-one else at the company who interacts with the honoree on a regular basis. Try to provide a cake or some great finger foods (your budget might be limited), and take up a small collection to buy the person a gift—request no more than $5 per person, and don't give anyone a hard time if they don't want to contribute. Even if you have little to spend, make the honoree's send-off special in some way; create a compila-tion CD, make a small scrapbook, or take the person to lunch at a nice restaurant. With the right attitude, you really can make any occasion a party.

Showers and Birthday Parties

These types of parties are of a personal nature, so in most companies it will be inap-propriate to have a birthday party or wedding or baby shower on company time. However, if your co-worker is expecting a child, planning a wedding, or celebrating a significant birthday, you and your co-workers will certainly wish to honor her. Either have the party after-hours, using funds collected from the other people in your department, or take the honoree out to lunch and gift her with presents. You can also have the party at your home; in this case, it is perfectly acceptable to split the costs and responsibilities of the party with one or more co-workers.

Summary

In this chapter, you learned how to plan parties for different occasions, including birthdays, showers, housewarming parties, and office occasions. In the next chapter, we'll take a look at parties you host purely for fun—parties at which the theme or entertainment takes center stage.

Throwing a Theme Party

11

In the two previous chapters, we looked at parties you'd give for a specific purpose, a holiday, or other special occasion. In this chapter, we'll look at parties whose only function is to entertain. Have these parties whenever you want—on a holiday or just because you feel like giving a party.

For each party, I'll give you a planning outline, including ideas for the date, theme, budget, venue, guest list, invitations, menu, décor, favors, music, and entertainment/activities. Although I'll outline each party to reflect a midrange budget, I'll include ideas about how to fancify or economize the event. You'll also see shopping and to-do lists for each party, which will help you get started on your planning.

As you read through these outlines, keep in mind your own party style. Whether you are classy or kitschy, modern or traditional, casual or formal, you will want to use your creativity and personal sense of style to plan the party *you* want to give.

Clever Costume Parties

Costume parties aren't just for Halloween. In fact, having an off-season costume party, such as in midsummer or the dead of winter, can be a lot of fun for your guests. Try one of these ideas for a costume party—and yes, if need be, you can have a costume party on Halloween.

note For recipes, please refer to the online chapters in Part V, "Eating and Drinking," at www.quepublishing.com.

You'll Need

- ❏ Ingredients for each of the recipes, as well as any serving or preparation tools
- ❏ Candles, dry ice, gauzy scarves, a crystal ball, pink and purple light bulbs, and incense
- ❏ Plain, palm-sized hand mirrors; craft pens, paints, glue, and/or decorations
- ❏ Professional or amateur psychic, fortuneteller, palmist, or seer
- ❏ Music CDs

Reincarnation Party: Come as You *Were*

A twist on the "come as you are" party, in which guests come wearing the attire suitable for whatever task they were performing just before the party (gardening, cooking, deep-sea diving), the "come as you *were*" party gives guests a chance to explore their past lives, real or imagined.

Costumes can run the gamut from the famous (Cleopatra, Marie Antoinette, Abraham Lincoln) to the quotidian (Grecian urn maker, Hopi Indian, fishwife). As long as guests can offer a believable explanation for their costume, they are complying with your party's theme.

Date, Theme, Budget, and Venue

Any weekend night—Because this party can occur at any time throughout the year, there really is no ideal date. Try to select a night in between holidays, so your guests won't be busy with other plans.

The supernatural is the theme—Play up the reincarnation theme with other supernatural elements, such as mystical décor and entertainment. Keep things light and avoid any décor or entertainment that is too morbid or occult.

Midrange budget—To do this party justice, you'll need to spend between $12 and $15 per person.

Party at home venue—Unless you can afford to rent out a banquet hall or other large, private space, have your party at home.

Guest List and Invitations

Invite 30 to 50 people to this party, including friends, family, and co-workers. Really, the more guests, the better the party, so invite as many guests as your budget will allow.

For a large, somewhat casual party, web-based invitations are best. You can customize your invites to reflect your theme and easily keep track of RSVPs.

Menu

Provide a wide selection of hearty foods in small portions. The tri-tip roast might seem an odd choice for a buffet, but this cut of meat is relatively inexpensive, and it's just as easy to cook three roasts as one. Plus, the meat falls apart easily, making it easy for guests to pile their plates high with tender, delicious meat.

- **Appetizers**—Prosciutto and Melon, Figs in a Blanket, Insalata Caprese (from the "Side Dishes" chapter; on the website at www.quepublishing.com), assorted cheeses and crackers, fresh fruit
- **Side dishes**—Caesar Salad to Go-Go, Sweet & Sour Cabbage, Brown-Buttered Butternut Squash, Herbed Garlic Bread
- **Main course**—Mom's Famous Tri-Tip Roast with Gravy, Green Grocer's Pasta Primavera
- **Dessert**—Pecan Pumpkin Pie, Beer Cake
- **Beverages**—Cranberry Cocktail Punch Cooler, Lemon Drops, Cosmopolitans, Classic Martinis

The pasta and assorted side dishes will provide an ample selection for your vegetarian guests. Also, providing a limited selection of cocktails allows you to offer your guests a varied assortment of drinks without requiring you to restock your bar.

Décor and Favors

Create a mystical, magical atmosphere with candles, dry ice, gauzy scarves (look at thrift stores), a crystal ball (gazing ball from a garden store), dim or colored lighting (pink and purple bulbs would work nicely), and incense. These items are all relatively inexpensive and can be found easily almost everywhere.

For favors, give out decorated hand mirrors, which guests can use to look into their past. You can find small, palm-sized hand mirrors for about $1 at import, novelty, or ethnic-specialty stores. Look for mirrors made from unfinished natural wood that you can decorate with craft paint, pens, stamps, or glued-on sequins and beads.

Music and Entertainment

Select haunting, ambient music for your party's soundtrack. Here are a few CDs that would work really well:

- *Passion*, Peter Gabriel
- *The Book of Secrets*, Loreena McKennitt
- *The K&D Sessions*, Kruder & Dorfmeister

Begin the party with smooth sounds; as the mood lifts, switch to ambient house music.

Consider hiring a professional psychic, tarot-card reader, or palmist for this party. Most professionals can give you a quote for the entire evening, and it might be lower than you imagine. Don't forget to tip your seer—10% to 15% of the total fee—and invite her to give your guests business cards, in case they enjoy her services enough to want another reading.

If you can't afford a professional seer, enlist one or more of your friends to perform at the party. A gypsy outfit (with head-scarf disguise), a crystal ball, a pack of tarot cards, a quiet corner or room, and above-average acting skills are all that your "psychic" needs to give an effective performance.

Other Creative Costume Parties

Apply this costume-party outline to any number of ideas to host a variety of silly, whimsical costume parties.

Tacky Party

At a tacky party, guests wear the tackiest outfits they can find—usually from thrift stores. Adjust your décor accordingly, piling cans of Spam into a pyramid and offering Cheez-Whiz, bologna, and Wonder Bread alongside your more appetizing fare. Your entertainment at this party might be a costume contest, and your favors should certainly be the tackiest knick-knacks you can find.

Decade Party

Pick a decade—'20s, '40s, '50s, '70s, or '80s—and build your party around it. Your invitations, décor, favors, and music should all reflect your chosen decade; your entertainment might be a dance contest from the era.

Indoor Beach Party

Bathing suits are the costumes at this super-easy party, although your guests can also dress as lifeguards or marine life, if they choose. Decorate your home with umbrellas and beach chairs and fire up the barbecue to roast some wieners and marshmallows. Your entertainment? Get out the limbo stick.

Gaming Parties

Games are good fun for guests of all ages. Instead of hosting a cocktail or dinner party, add a little fun and games to the mix.

You'll Need

- ❑ Ingredients for each of the recipes, as well as preparation tools and serving dishes
- ❑ Music
- ❑ Dice prizes
- ❑ A pair of dice

Dice Party

Some call it "bunko"; others insist it's a "white elephant" party. In my parlance, the game is dice, and it's the most popular party with my posse.

Date, Theme, Budget, and Venue

Any weekend night—No occasion is necessary to host a dice party, but feel free to combine this activity with a holiday party. Begin the dice party at 8:00 p.m.

No theme required—It's all about the dice game, baby.

Low budget—You won't need to spend much more than $5 to $8 per person.

Your home venue—You'll need a large, open space for this party; if you have a good-sized dining-room table, move it to the living room. Otherwise, plan for guests to sit on the floor in the living room or on the grass in the backyard. You'll want your guests to form a large circle, leaving room in the middle for displaying prizes and tossing dice.

Guest List and Invitations

Invite as many people as you'd like to this fun party, including friends, friends-of-friends, acquaintances, and co-workers. The more, the merrier!

Use web-based invitations for this casual party. It's essential that your friends understand the rules and theory of the dice game, so be sure to include specific instructions on your invitations.

Menu

Party food, simple and light, is perfect for this cocktail-party-with-a-twist.

- **Appetizers**—Deviled Eggs, Grandma's Chicken Wings, Prosciutto and Melon, Dee's Bean Dip, Iptacita's Guacamole, tortilla chips
- **Side dishes**—Zuchinni-Walnut Bread, Terry Wilkinson's Summer Salad, Mediterranean Pasta
- **Dessert**—Lemon-Poppyseed Cakebread (make a large loaf and cut into small pieces), fudge, assorted cookies
- **Beverages**—Mexican Coffee, assorted soda, bottled water

Because you need to keep your wits about you to snag the best prize, this party works well as a sober party. Add "BYOB" to your invitations so guests know you won't be providing alcohol.

Décor and Favors

One of the best things about this party is that no décor or favors are required. Your guests are there for two reasons: to eat and to play dice. Don't mess around with fancy extras that will go largely ignored.

Music and Entertainment

Throw a selection of upbeat, popular music into the CD player, but turn off the tunes when the dice game begins.

Miss Betty's Dice Game is all about kitsch: Guests roll the dice to vie for tacky prizes they can then steal from one another. For complete rules, see the sidebar, "Miss Betty's Dice Game."

MISS BETTY'S DICE GAME

Number of players: 10 to 30

Objective: To get the "best" prize

In a nutshell: Players take turns rolling two dice. A roll of doubles earns a prize. In the first round, select a new prize from the pool in the center of the playing area; in the second round, steal someone else's already-won prize. The game ends when the timer goes off (set it for 30 minutes before you begin to play).

Prizes: Before playing, have a prize parade, in which guests show off the prizes they've brought (everyone *must bring* at least one prize), and try to convince the other players that they really must have the item. Prizes needn't be wrapped or otherwise obscured—unless you'd like them to be secret prizes. Large prizes can be put into play with a representational index card.

The best kinds of prizes are kitschy, kooky toys and stuff. Examples include

- ✳ A screaming Macaulay Culkin doll from *Home Alone*
- ✳ A box of new-wave pins from the '80s
- ✳ An original paint-by-number portrait of a cat with big, sorrowful eyes
- ✳ A really horrible "Snow White" piñata
- ✳ The Britney Spears Action Tour Bus, complete with microphone
- ✳ A pink, crystal unicorn music box
- ✳ Nearly anything from the '70s

Tailor prizes to your crowd, making them more or less offensive according to how much the prizes will make your friends laugh.

How to play: Have guests sit in a circle. After the prize parade, have guests place their prizes in the center of the circle. The game is played in two rounds: The first round ends when all the prizes have been claimed from the center of the circle. The second round is timed—20 to 30 minutes is a good amount of time.

Each player rolls a pair of dice. If the player gets doubles, he gets to take whatever prize he likes from the center. This continues until all the prizes are gone. The players must display their prizes so they are clearly visible to everyone. No hiding of prizes is allowed, but subtle subterfuge is encouraged (such as wearing a piece of jewelry or clothing, or sitting on a large box full of *Mad* magazines). Be sneaky.

For the next round, continue around the circle, with each player rolling dice. The next player to roll doubles can take the prize she likes from the player who has it. This is how "Star Prizes" are born. Certain prizes become eminently desirable to just about everyone and, until the timer runs out, these prizes will get pulled all over the circle. There might be bloodshed and name-calling, but it's all in good fun. All's fair in love and dice.

As the screams, pleas, and directives from the players increase in intensity, the timer starts to run out. When it buzzes, rings, dings, or whatever, the game is *over*. No trades. No crying. The end. Players who are stuck with a prize they truly despise are encouraged to disguise it and bring it to the next game.

More Ideas for Fun and Games

After you've begun to throw game-based parties, you might find you prefer them to more traditional get-togethers. No worries; there are plenty of gaming parties to host.

Games Night

Enhance a dinner party for six with an evening of game playing. After serving a delicious sit-down dinner for two other couples, bust out the games: Pictionary, Cranium, Trivial Pursuit, and Settlers of Catan all work well. Take a break after an hour of playing and enjoy coffee and dessert. This casual dinner party is perfect for entertaining new friends.

Scavenger Hunt

One of the more traditional party games, scavenger hunts can be adapted to any number of scenarios:

- Citywide scavenger hunt for teams of three to five players; select odd and imaginative items for this game
- Movie scavenger hunt (you'll need a room and a DVD or video player for each team), wherein guests cite the movie or scene from which obscure quotes are pulled
- Clue-based scavenger hunt, which involves players figuring out successive clues that lead to a fabulous party at the end of the game

At each of these parties, the game itself is the main event; no décor or favors are really necessary. Plan a cocktail party with finger food at the end of the game, and don't forget to offer prizes for teams that finish first, second, and third.

Sports Party

Host a party around an annual or significant sports event, such as the Super Bowl, the Kentucky Derby, the Indianapolis 500, or an important boxing match. Skip the décor and favors and focus on event-appropriate food and drink: football-shaped sandwiches for Super Bowl Sunday; Mint Juleps for Derby Day.

Entertainment *Is* the Party

Some of the best parties are focused around a specific form of entertainment, such as reading and discussing a book, viewing and analyzing a movie, or exploring a common interest, such as cooking or traveling. Along these lines is my favorite party, the dog party.

You'll Need

- ❏ Ingredients for each of the recipes, as well as preparation and serving tools
- ❏ Bowls for water
- ❏ Treat bags for favors
- ❏ Liver cake (see sidebar)

Pet-Together

A pet-together is a wonderful way for humans to interact while their pets socialize. Although this party is called a "pet-together" (a play on "get-together"), the only pets it really works with are dogs. Cats tend to be too territorial, and birds and reptiles aren't that social. However, any pet lovers are welcome at this party; hence its name.

Date, Theme, Budget, and Venue

Any weekend afternoon—There's no need to tie in this party to a holiday. Host your pet-together at about 2:00 p.m. on a Saturday or a Sunday.

Pet theme—Although most of your guests will be dog people, many of your guests will have other pets, as well: cats, rabbits, reptiles, gerbils, hamsters, and birds. Keep these different species in mind if you decide to decorate.

Low to midrange budget—You have a little budget flexibility with a pet-together; keep your food and favors simple, and you can price the party at $5 a person. Opt for more extravagant food and favors and you can spend up to $12 a person.

Your backyard venue—Although you might be tempted to host the pet-together at a dog park, remember you can't bring food or dog treats there. Tidy your backyard, removing anything poisonous to animals, and make sure you have plenty of water available for your canine guests.

Guest List and Invitations

A pet-together is a great way to deepen your friendships with people you've met at the dog park, around the neighborhood, or while you're out walking your dog. Invite people and pets that appeal to both you and your dog, limiting the guest list to about a dozen people. The ratio of humans to dogs should be 1:1, so if a guest wants to bring more than one dog, he should also bring a friend to monitor that dog.

Invitations should be casual—given the nature of the guest list, you might not have all your guests' email addresses, so a web-based invitation system probably won't work. Instead, make up flyers that list all the pertinent information: date, time, location, and house rules (any dog size limits). Keep a few flyers with you during the weeks before the pet-together so you can give one to people you regularly encounter while spending time with your dog.

Menu

Although the pets are the guests of honor at this party, humans need to eat, too. Serve this simple menu (make sure the table is high enough to remain off-limits to pooches):

- **Appetizers**—Seven-Layer Traveling Taco Dip and tortilla chips, Classic Spinach Dip, Mostly Fresh Fruit Salad (from the "Side Dishes" online chapter), Stuffed Mushrooms
- **Dessert**—Beer Cake (for the humans), Liver Cake (for the dogs—see sidebar)
- **Beverages**—Very Berry Lemonade, assorted soda, bottled water, coffee, and tea

If you have a little more to spend, purchase a customized sheet cake decorated with images of different pets: cats, dogs, horses, rabbits, reptiles, and birds.

Because chocolate is tempting (and poisonous!) to dogs, don't serve any desserts made with it.

Décor and Favors

You don't really need to decorate for this party, but if you want, you can get pet-themed paper plates, napkins, tablecloths, or other décor. Do make sure your backyard is clean and free of anything you don't want a bunch of strange dogs to maul, such as expensive pottery, delicate potted plants, or cats.

For favors, give out doggie goodie bags that include a roll of doo-doo bags (sold at pet stores in lots of six rolls), homemade or fancy pet cookies, a small squeaky toy, and a chew treat. Use plain brown paper bags, or purchase drawstring bags to hold the treats. Make sure to make up a few extra bags for unexpected guests.

Music and Entertainment

You won't really need any music, and the dogs are the entertainment. If you'd like, set out a boom box with peppy music in case conversation wanes.

You'll want to observe a few common-sense safety rules:

- Keep dogs on leash until they've had a chance to sniff one another. After they've said hello, let them romp free in the backyard.

- Make sure that each guest keeps an eye on his dog throughout the party. If a guest needs a bathroom break, offer to watch his pooch while he's in the house.

- If a canine seems over-stimulated or hyper, he might need a timeout. Direct the guest to a quiet area where she and her dog can take five.

- Pick up any pet waste immediately; some dogs eat other dogs' doo-doo.

> **tip** Purchase an airhorn for the party. The loud, sudden noise will break up any squabbles the dogs get into. Also, have the hose handy as a backup brawl-buster.

LIVER CAKE RECIPE

1 lb. raw liver

1 C cornmeal

1 T wheat germ

4 eggs

Garlic to taste

Softened cream cheese or peanut butter

Preheat oven to 350 degrees. Put raw liver into a food processor or blender until liver is almost liquefied. Combine all ingredients in a large mixing bowl. Fold into a greased cake pan and bake for 30 minutes. Allow to cool, and frost with cream cheese or peanut butter. Serves 6 dogs.

More Group Gatherings

Using the same menu and attitude, you can host a number of other entertainment-based parties. Make these events regular, monthly, or bimonthly occurrences, taking place at the different group members' homes.

Cooking Group

This group can work two ways: The month before, you select a menu and prepare the meal together, sharing the cost of ingredients; or, each guest brings a different dish on the menu and you eat together as a group. Either way, explore different cuisine from around the world; exotic locations such as Burma, Spain, and Morocco offer tasty dishes that are surprisingly simple to prepare.

Film Group

Although HBO's *The Sopranos* didn't make an American Film Institute Top 100 Party look very fun, your film party needn't be a drag. Get together with a dozen friends who enjoy discussing films, and rent a movie from the Top 100 list. Watch it together and discuss the film afterward. The host should research and prepare a short list of questions to get the conversation flowing, and the group members should potluck it and bring different snacks to share.

Book Club

A book club or reading group takes place once or twice a month at a cafe or at different group members' homes. The host should prepare a meal or provide the basics for a potluck (beverages, serving tools and dishes, and a dessert) and be prepared to lead a discussion of the book. The members should select the title at the previous meeting; everyone needs to have read the book before the meeting begins. Each reading group should have the same sort of books in mind: biographies/memoirs, thrillers/mysteries, politics/history, science/nature, or contemporary fiction/literature.

"Girly" Parties

Although anyone can attend a "girly" party, these events (also known as a "stitch and bitch") are really intended as a forum for women to get together and complain about their significant others as they enjoy one another's company.

You'll Need

- ❏ Ingredients for each of the recipes, as well as any cooking and serving tools
- ❏ Materials for the craft project
- ❏ Music CDs

Craft Party

Hosting a craft party gives you two benefits: You'll meet other women who enjoy your same pursuits, and you'll learn more about how to do a particular craft.

Date, Theme, Budget, and Venue

Any weekend afternoon or evening—As you gather members in your group, discuss what times and days of the week will work best. If this is your first time meeting, schedule the initial group for a weekend afternoon, beginning at about 1:00 p.m.

No theme—In order for this regular group meeting to be a success, you'll want to keep things simple. Forgo a theme and the associated décor and favors.

Low budget—You shouldn't spend more than $5 to $7 per person, including food and supplies.

Your home venue—Although a craft group can work well at a cafe or library, your best bet is to host the group at your home (subsequent meetings can revolve around other members' homes), where you have an ample store of cleaning supplies.

Guest List and Invitations

Finding guests who are interested in crafting might seem difficult at first, but with a little ingenuity, you can find about 8 to 12 people interested in a particular project. Ask around at your work, church, dog park, neighborhood, school, or other social group. You might also post a listing on a community or Internet bulletin board. If you can only find a few members at first, don't despair; successful groups have a tendency to thrive, and your membership should expand accordingly.

Use Internet-based invitations to provide guests with all the information they'll need: time, date, location, and supplies they'll need to bring.

Menu

Either host a potluck or provide a simple spread—there's no need to get fancy with the menu for this party.

- **Appetizers**—Classic Spinach Dip, assorted cheeses, fruit, and crackers
- **Dessert**—Cream Cheese Brownies
- **Beverages**—Soda, water, and coffee or tea

To add an elegant touch to your gathering, visit a bakery and pick up a scrumptious cake or torte to serve while you're waiting for the paint to dry.

If your group takes off and you meet regularly, you can always discuss changes to the menu; you might want to have the host prepare a main dish, with each member bringing a side dish, dessert, or beverage.

Décor and Favors

No décor or favors are necessary; provide a clean, organized home and a flat work surface for projects.

Music and Entertainment

As you're crafting, you might want to listen to mellow vocals, jazz, or classical music. Here are a few of my favorites:

- *The Essential Nina Simone*, Nina Simone
- *Come Away with Me*, Norah Jones
- *Seal IV*, Seal

Keep the sound low enough to talk over; the music should serve as a background for your conversation.

The entertainment is the focus of this party: your craft project. Browse online or visit craft stores for ideas. You'll want a beginner-level project that can be completed in about three or four hours. See the sidebar for an idea to get you started.

You can also work on knitting, crochet, cross-stitch, embroidery, needlepoint, quilting, or sewing projects. These types of projects are great for people of all experience levels; by working on a group project or working together on solo projects, you can learn from one another and improve your skills.

> **tip** If your group has trouble thinking of crafts to do, make simple holiday decorations for donation to children's or senior homes. You'll feel good about your creations, knowing that less fortunate people will be able to enjoy them. For craft ideas, check out a couple of craft books from your local library or perform some Internet research.

PAINTING TERRA-COTTA POTS

Painting terra-cotta pots is a simple, fun craft that anyone can do successfully. Guests will need to bring their own pots, but you can provide the additional materials:

* ❋ Craft paints and pens in a variety of colors
* ❋ Paintbrushes with small tips
* ❋ Sponge brushes in a variety of sizes
* ❋ Stencils in a variety of patterns
* ❋ Vinyl letters in a couple of sizes
* ❋ Glaze or sealant spray

This project could not be simpler! Using paints and pens, decorate the pots with designs that appeal to your personal aesthetic. You might want to purchase a book of patterns to get you started, or download ideas from the Internet.

You can also paint on one layer, let it dry, apply letters or stencils, and paint on another layer. Remove the vinyl letters when the paint is completely dry.

When the pots are dry—you'll only need to wait an hour or so—spray them with glaze or sealant spray.

More Girly Fun

Crafts and needlework aren't the only reasons women get together and bond. You can apply the same party outline to other concepts for female bonding, such as a beauty night or a product party.

Beauty Night

Gather together a few good friends for a night of facials, manicures and pedicures, hair treatments, and make-up experimentation. If you're female, you probably indulged in beauty nights in high school, but chances are good you haven't had a beauty night since graduation. Indulge in a night all to yourself (ship off the husband and/or kids to a double feature) and the ladies. While you're getting beautiful, throw on a classic chick flick or two, such as one of the following:

* *Dirty Dancing*
* *Grease*
* *When Harry Met Sally*
* *Xanadu*

- *Chicago*
- *Pretty Woman*
- *Say Anything*
- *Breakfast at Tiffany's*
- *Bridget Jones's Diary*
- *Legally Blonde*

Don't share make-up (bacteria and germs), but feel free to swap polish and facial and hair products. Serve booze if you'd like; if the party takes off, you might wind up hosting a sleepover.

Product Party

Traditionally, Avon, Mary Kay, and Tupperware have been common products sold at "parties," events many a woman has been tricked into attending. However, the modern spin on these parties includes more interesting products: candles, holiday décor, housewares, kitchen gadgets, lingerie, even sex toys! If you'd like to host a product party, observe a few rules of etiquette:

- Don't trick your guests into attending. Do not promise them "free" makeovers or anything of the like. Inform them that you are hosting a product party, and you would love for them to attend. No other persuasion is necessary.
- Don't pressure your guests into buying anything. If they want to buy things, they will. If they don't, please do not make them feel bad.
- Make the party fun. Although the goal of these parties is usually to make money, you'll need to switch your focus to the guests' perspective and make sure the guests have fun. Offer good food, ample beverages, and an inviting atmosphere.

Don't host more than one product party a year, lest your friends think you a hostess with an ulterior motive. Make these evenings fun, and focus on sharing new ideas and products with your friends.

Summary

In this chapter, we looked at a variety of theme parties, including costume parties, gaming parties, entertainment-based parties, and girly parties. This chapter marks the end of *Plan a Fabulous Party In No Time*. I hope you have enjoyed the book!

Part IV

Party Planning Tools

References and Resources

Stores

Although you can find great deals on party supplies, food, beverages, and tools at these stores—most of which have locations nationwide—you'll want to check your own area for additional discount grocery, houseware, and party stores.

Costco
800-774-2678
www.costco.com

Ikea
888-966-4532
www.ikea.com

Sam's Club
888-746-7726
www.samsclub.com

Target
800-440-0680
www.target.com

Trader Joe's
800-SHOP-TJS
www.traderjoes.com

Wal-Mart
800-WAL-MART
www.walmart.com

KMART
866-562-7848
www.kmart.com

Cost Plus World Market
510-893-7300
www.costplus.com

Party City
973-983-0888
www.partycity.com

Books

Although you can find almost anything you need on the Internet, it's smart to build a resource library of expert opinions on a variety of entertaining subjects. In addition to my book, consider adding these volumes:

The Best Bachelorette Party Book, Becky Long (Meadowbrook Press, 2000)

The Playboy Guide to Bachelor Parties: Everything You Need to Know About Planning the Groom's Rite of Passage—From Simple to Sinful, James Oliver Cury (Fireside Books, 2003)

The Best Wedding Shower Book: A Complete Guide for Party Planners, Courtney Cooke (Meadowbrook Press, 2001)

Themed Baby Showers: Mother Goose to Noah's Ark: Hundreds of Creative Shower Ideas, Becky Long (Meadowbrook Press, 2003)

The Penny Whistle Birthday Party Book, Meredith Brokaw, Annie Gilbar, and Jill Weber (Fireside Books, 1992)

Memorable Milestone Birthdays: 48 Theme Parties to Help You Celebrate, Robin Kring (Meadowbrook Press, 2001)

An Anniversary to Remember: Years One to Seventy-Five, Cynthia Lueck Sowden (Brighton Publications, 1992)

Event Planning: The Ultimate Guide to Successful Meetings, Corporate Events, Fundraising Galas, Conferences, Conventions, Incentives and Other Special Events, Judy Allen (John Wiley & Sons, 2000)

The Ultimate Party Drink Book: Over 750 Recipes for Cocktails, Smoothies, Blender Drinks, Non-Alcoholic Drinks, and More, Bruce Weinstein (Morrow Cookbooks, 2000)

Celebrate!, Sheila Lukins (Workman Publishing, 2003)

The $50 Dinner Party: 26 Dinner Parties That Won't Break Your Bank, Your Back or Your Schedule, Sally Sampson (Fireside Books, 1998)

50 Easy Party Cakes, Debbie Brown (Whitecap Books, 2000)

Traditional Holiday Ethnic Recipes: Collected All Over the World, Duane Lund (Adventure Publications, 1998)

Perfect Party Games, Andrea Campbell and Sanford Hoffman (Sterling Publishing, 2001)

The New Decorating Book, Better Homes and Gardens (Better Homes and Gardens Books, 2001)

Making a Home: Housekeeping for Real Life, Better Homes and Gardens (Better Homes and Gardens Books, 2001)

Checklists for Life: 104 Lists to Help You Get Organized, Save Time, and Unclutter Your Life, Kirsten M. Lagatree (Random House Reference Publishing, 2000)

The Good Housekeeping Illustrated Cookbook (Hearst Books, 2001)

How to Cook Everything: Simple Recipes for Great Food, Mark Bittman (Wiley, 1998)

Weber's Big Book of Grilling, Jamie Purviance (Chronicle Books, 2001)

Mr. Boston: Official Bartender's and Party Guide, Renee Cooper and Chris Morris (Warner Books, 2000)

Emily Post's Entertaining, Peggy Post (HarperResource, 1998)

Party Tools

Throughout this book, I offered plenty of advice on planning a party. In this appendix, I'll give you all the planning tools you'll need to pull off your gala event, beginning with a well-stocked kitchen.

To Have on Hand

Before you become a bona fide cruise director, make sure you have a few essentials on hand. You don't have to rush right out and buy everything on this list—accumulate items over time until your cupboards are no longer bare.

Equipment

It's important to purchase good-quality equipment, especially when it comes to pots and pans. However, cooking equipment can be expensive, so unless you're the beneficiary of a wedding registry, shop discount stores, where you can often find quality pieces at reduced prices.

- Baking pan, 11"×17" stainless steel
- Baking pan, 8"×8" stainless steel
- Baking sheets, 2
- Cake pans, 2
- Casserole dish, 8"×8" glass
- Casserole dish, 9"×13" glass

- Cutting board, plastic (for meat)
- Cutting board, wood
- Double boiler
- Griddle, cast iron
- Loaf pan, glass
- Loaf pan, metal
- Pie pans, 2
- Pizza pan
- Pot, 4-quart with lid
- Saucepan, 1-quart with lid
- Saucepan, 2-quart with lid
- Skillet, 10" cast-iron
- Skillet, 10" stainless steel
- Skillet, 12"
- Skillet, 6"
- Stockpot, 8-quart with lid
- Wire cooling racks, 2
- Wok

Electronics

Although it was once important to spend a fair amount of money on quality kitchen electronics, many of the items on this list are now available at much lower prices from bargain stores, such as Wal-Mart or Target. Unless you are a coffee or smoothie junkie, there's really no reason to spend $300 on a blender or coffee maker. Purchase mid-priced electronics that will last several years, and you'll be fine.

- Blender
- Bread machine
- Coffee maker
- Food processor
- Microwave oven
- Mixer
- Toaster oven

Gadgets

Kitchen gadgets, which don't have to cost more than a few dollars each, are really great to have in the kitchen. Sure, you don't really need an apple corer if you have a good knife, but they are so much fun to use—and so inexpensive!—that I don't see any reason why you can't spend a lovely afternoon in your local dollar store, stocking up on tools that will make your cooking life easier.

- Apple corer
- Baster
- Bottle opener
- Can opener
- Colander
- Flour sifter
- Fork, long-handled meat
- Funnel
- Garlic press
- Grater
- Juicer
- Kitchen scale
- Kitchen scissors
- Kitchen timer
- Knife, 11" serrated
- Knife, 4" paring
- Knife, 8" chef's
- Ladle
- Measuring cups, dry
- Measuring cups, liquid
- Measuring spoons
- Meat tenderizer
- Meat thermometer, digital
- Melon baller
- Mixing bowls, glass
- Mixing bowls, stainless steel
- Pancake turner
- Pastry brush
- Pizza cutter
- Plastic storage containers
- Potato masher
- Rolling pin
- Skewers, metal
- Skewers, wooden
- Slotted spoon
- Spatula, metal
- Spatula, rubber
- Teakettle
- Tongs
- Toothpicks
- Twine
- Vegetable peeler
- Whisk
- Wooden spoons (assorted sizes)
- Zester

Pantry

Your wallet will complain less if you buy two bottles of spices a week for 10 weeks, as opposed to 20 bottles in one week. Spices generally only retain their efficacy for one to two years, so be sure to rotate the contents of your spice cabinet accordingly.

- Baking powder
- Baking soda
- Beans, canned black
- Beans, canned pinto
- Beans, canned refried
- Bouillon, beef
- Bouillon, chicken
- Bread crumbs
- Chocolate, bittersweet/baking
- Chocolate, chips
- Cocoa/chocolate powder
- Coffee, whole bean
- Coffee, whole bean decaffeinated
- Cornstarch
- Couscous
- Cream of mushroom soup
- Extract, peppermint
- Extract, vanilla
- Flour, white
- Fruit, raisins
- Honey
- Milk, canned condensed
- Milk, canned evaporated
- Milk, powdered
- Nuts, chopped walnuts
- Oil, extra-virgin olive
- Oil, peanut
- Oil, sesame
- Oil, vegetable

- Pasta, angel hair
- Pasta, farfalle
- Pasta, rotelli
- Pasta, spaghetti
- Peanut butter
- Rice, brown
- Rice, white
- Salad dressing, Italian
- Salsa
- Salt, kosher or sea
- Salt, table
- Sauce, barbecue
- Sauce, hot
- Sauce, marinara
- Sauce, soy
- Sauce, teriyaki
- Sauce, Worcestershire
- Spices, basil
- Spices, bay leaves
- Spices, caraway seeds
- Spices, celery seeds
- Spices, chili powder
- Spices, cinnamon
- Spices, cloves
- Spices, cumin
- Spices, curry
- Spices, dill weed
- Spices, ginger
- Spices, marjoram

- Spices, mint
- Spices, mustard
- Spices, nutmeg
- Spices, oregano
- Spices, paprika
- Spices, pepper, black
- Spices, pepper, crushed red flakes
- Spices, pepper, white
- Spices, pickling
- Spices, poppyseeds
- Spices, rosemary
- Spices, sage
- Spices, sesame seeds
- Spices, tarragon
- Spices, cream of tartar
- Spices, thyme
- Stock, beef
- Stock, chicken
- Stock, vegetable
- Sugar substitute
- Sugar, brown
- Sugar, cubes
- Sugar, granulated
- Sugar, powdered
- Syrup, maple
- Tea, assorted bags

- Tomato paste
- Tomato sauce
- Tuna
- Vegetables (canned), corn
- Vegetables (canned), green chilies
- Vegetables (canned), stewed tomatoes
- Vegetables (canned), whole tomatoes
- Vegetables (marinated), artichoke hearts
- Vegetables (marinated), capers
- Vegetables (marinated), mushrooms
- Vegetables (marinated), olives
- Vegetables (marinated), roasted red peppers
- Vegetables (marinated), sun-dried tomatoes
- Vinegar, balsamic
- Vinegar, cider
- Vinegar, red wine
- Vinegar, rice
- Vinegar, white
- Vinegar, white wine
- Wine, sherry
- Wine, white

Freezer

Although I've only included a bare-minimum freezer list, feel free to fill your freezer as space allows with meat, frozen fruits and vegetables, and other quickly prepared items for parties and daily life. For example, if your grocery store is having a special on veggie burgers, pick up a package or two, and you'll always be able to accommodate your vegetarian guests.

- Fruit, raspberries
- Fruit, strawberries
- Ice cubes
- Orange juice concentrate
- Veggie burgers
- Whipped topping

Refrigerator

Although you can't keep fresh produce in the refrigerator forever, you *can* stock up on sauces, dressings, and condiments as they go on sale, ensuring you'll be able to top any burger at a moment's notice.

- Butter
- Cheese, cream
- Cheese, Parmesan
- Eggs
- Half-and-half
- Horseradish
- Jams/Preserves
- Ketchup
- Mayonnaise
- Milk (lowfat, soy)
- Mustard, Dijon
- Mustard, rough
- Mustard, spicy/deli
- Mustard, yellow
- Sour cream
- Yogurt, plain

Linen Cabinet

Scour discount stores for quality linens, and you won't have to spend a fortune stocking your linen cabinet. Before storing, wash and iron each item, fold carefully, and you'll be ready for any occasion (a tablecloth with creases is acceptable on any table).

- Tablecloth, white fabric
- Tablecloth, patterned fabric
- Napkins, white fabric, 12

Serveware

If you're just starting out, make sure you get at least one serving bowl, platter, and tray—a neutral color, such as white, will ensure your platters complement your dishes for many years to come. As you fill in your serveware blanks, look at discount stores for fun dishes in large sizes, and don't be afraid to use a little creativity: An oversized pasta bowl will look lovely filled with fresh fruit.

- Cheese board
- Pitchers, glass
- Platters, large
- Punch bowl, cups, and ladle
- Serving bowls, large
- Serving trays
- Utensils: serving ladle, meat fork, and serving spoons

Other Essentials

Having these items on hand will make your life easier. For "summer" items, shop in July or August for great bargains. Don't forget discount stores for candles, note cards, and vases!

- Vases, assorted sizes and colors
- Barware: jigger, shaker, and ice bucket
- Candles, assorted sizes and colors
- Picnic blanket
- Picnic basket
- Blank note cards (for invitations and thank-you notes)
- Party games: Trivial Pursuit, Pictionary, Cranium, Scrabble, Uno, Yahtzee!, decks of cards, and dice

Food and Drink Calculator

To determine how many drinks and portions of food you'll need, simply fill in this handy little chart. Use your total number of guests as a multiplier, assuming that although not everyone will consume as much as you plan to serve, others will consume more. After you've determined your total portions, you can do the math with each recipe you select.

Course	# Guests	Total
Beverages		
2/person/hour for first 2 hours	_____	_____
1/person/hour thereafter	_____	_____
½ lb. ice/person	_____	_____
Appetizers		
5 servings/person/hour for first 2 hours	_____	_____
3 servings/person/hour thereafter (until dinner is served)	_____	_____
Side Dishes		
Bread: 1 serving/person	_____	_____
Salad: 1 serving/person	_____	_____
Vegetable: 1 serving/person	_____	_____
Grain: 1 serving/person	_____	_____
Main Course		
1.5 servings/person	_____	_____
Dessert		
1 serving/person	_____	_____
Coffee		
1 serving/person	_____	_____

Budget Planner

In Chapter 5, "Planning Ahead," we used a nifty chart to track each of our budget expenses. Here is that chart—copy it or create your own version on your computer.

Element	Cost
Total Budget	$
Invitations	$
Venue	$
Food	$
Drink	$
Tools	$
Décor	$
Entertainment/Activities	$
Music	$
Favors	$
Emergency Fund	$
Total Costs	$

Task List

This master task list can guide you through almost any type of party. Photocopy it, or make a copy on your computer that you can customize for your own parties.

✔	Task
	Set date and time
	Select venue
	Decide theme
	Select guest list
	Determine budget
	Send out invitations
	Plan menu
	Select beverages
	Determine what tools you'll need
	Select décor
	Plan entertainment or activities
	Select music
	Select favors
	Schedule time
	Go shopping
	Clean house
	Tidy yard/entry area
	Prepare food
	Decorate house
	Get yourself ready

Grocery Shopping

Use this grocery list to help you determine which ingredients you need to purchase from what store. Photocopy it, or make a copy on your computer that you can customize for your own parties.

✔	Ingredients	Quantity	$	Store

Index

C

F

S

T

U - V

W - Z

Do Even More ...In No Time

Must See

Get ready to cross off those items on your to-do list! *In No Time* helps you tackle the projects that you don't think you have time to finish. With shopping lists and step-by-step instructions, these books get you working toward accomplishing your goals.

Check out these other *In No Time* books, coming soon!

Start Your Own Home Business In No Time
ISBN: **0-7897-3224-6**
$16.95
September 2004

Plan a Fabulous Party In No Time
ISBN: **0-7897-3221-1**
$16.95
September 2004

Speak Basic Spanish In No Time
ISBN: **0-7897-3223-8**
$16.95
September 2004

Organize Your Garage In No Time
ISBN: **0-7897-3219-X**
$16.95
October 2004

Quick Family Meals In No Time
ISBN: **0-7897-3299-8**
$16.95
October 2004

Organize Your Family's Schedule In No Time
ISBN: **0-7897-3220-3**
$16.95
October 2004